The
Aborigines

Linda Reed

The Aborigines

R.M. Gibbs

Longman Cheshire

Longman Cheshire Pty Limited
Longman House
Kings Gardens
95 Coventry Street
Melbourne 3205 Australia

Associated companies, branches, and representatives throughout the world. Offices in Sydney, Brisbane, Adelaide, and Perth.

First published 1974
Reprinted 1975, 1977, 1979, 1981
Second Edition 1982
Reprinted 1984, 1986

Produced by Longman Cheshire Pty Limited
Printed in Hong Kong

National Library of Australia
Cataloguing-in-Publication data

Gibbs, R. M. (Ronald Malcolm), 1938–
   The Aborigines.

   2nd ed.
   Previous ed.: Hawthorn, Vic.: Longman, 1974.
   For secondary school students.
   Bibliography.
   Includes index.
   ISBN 0 582 66531 0.

   [1]. Aborigines, Australian. I. Title.

994'.0049915

Preface

This book is an attempt to provide an introduction to the origin and culture of the Aboriginal people of Australia. It also gives some account of the impact of white settlement on the Aborigines. It does not, however, provide a highly detailed study of Aboriginal society, nor a comprehensive study of relations between white and black—the reading list elsewhere suggests books that will do that. Its purpose is to encourage a student or general reader to ask questions: above all, what kind of society did Aborigines create in Australia, and what has happened to it?

The author wishes to acknowledge the valuable suggestions and comments of Professor C. M. Tatz, Mr R. M. Shanahan, and Mr I. Spalding, and especially the generosity of time and talent of Robert Edwards, formerly Curator of Anthropology at the South Australian Museum.

Acknowledgements

Acknowledgement is due to the following sources for permission to reproduce material in this book: Mr Robert Edwards for photographs on pages 2, 3, 14, 30, 32, 33, 36, 40, 41, 43, 46, 57, 62, 63, 67, 68, 69, 70, 71, 73 and 74; *The Advertiser* Adelaide for the extract on page 17 and photograph on p. 111; The South Australian Archives for illustrations on pages 19, 22, 31, 48, 58, 95, 96, 97, 98 and 101; *The News* Adelaide for photographs on pages 104, 107, 109, 113, 116, 117, 118, and 119; the La Trobe Library Melbourne for illustrations on pages 57, 90 and 91; J. W. Beattie for photographs on pages 83 and 89; The State Library of South Australia for illustrations on pages 7, 23, 60, 80 and 84, and for the extracts from the Journals of Eyre, Sturt, and Grey; The Australian and New Zealand Association for the Advancement of Science for illustrations on page 13; A. H. and A. W. Reed Ltd for illustrations on pages 21, 25, 29, 39, 42, 49, 61 and 65; John Currey O'Neill Pty Ltd for illustrations on pages 27, 33, 35, 36, 37, 49, 59, 67 and 90; Ernest Benn Ltd for photographs on pages 22 and 37; Angus and Robertson (Publishers) Pty Ltd for three illustrations and the legend 'How the Sun was Made' on pages 20, 27, 35, 52 and 55–6; Macmillan, London and Basingstoke for illustrations on pages 46 and 64; Jacaranda Press for the poem 'A Song of Hope' by Kath Walker; Fuller's Bookshop Hobart for the illustrations on page 13; Professor D. J. Mulvaney for the illustration on page 3; Mr C. J. Hackett for the illustration on page 39; West Australian Newspapers Ltd for the illustration on page 121; and Mr George Burnell for the illustration on page 43; M. Gallagher for photographs on page 111; Australian Information Service for photograph on page 114.

Contents

Map of Australia, showing some archaeological sites, tribal areas and localities mentioned in the text

Melville Island
Tiwi tribe
Bathurst Island
Darwin
Larakia tribe
Yirrkala
Caledon Bay
Arnhem Land
Groote Eylandt
Roper River
Wyndham
Delamere
Kimberley Ra.
Victoria River
Wave Hill
Djingili tribe
NORTHERN TERRITORY
Cairns
Rockingham Bay
QUEENSLAND
Wailbri tribe
Warramunga tribe
WESTERN AUSTRALIA
Barrow Creek
Cleland Hills
Alice Springs
Aranda tribe
Kenniff Cave
Gibson Desert
Pitjantjatjara tribe
James Ra.
Ayers Rock
Musgrave Ra.
Moreton Bay
Ernabella
Indulkana
Brewarinna
Brisbane
Wiluna
Birksgate Ra.
Everard Ra.
Cooper
Creek
Talgai
Mt Margaret Mission
SOUTH AUSTRALIA
Lake Eyre
Lake Callabonna
Grafton
Macquarie River
Myall Creek
Nullarbor Plain
L. Torrens
Mootwingee
Darling River
NEW SOUTH WALES
Mirning tribe
Port Augusta
Lake Menindee
Fraser Ra.
Koonalda Cave
Fromm's Landing
Lachlan River
Lapstone Creek
Perth
Pinjarra
Adelaide
Rapid Bay
Lake Mungo
Sydney
Bibalman tribe
Kangaroo Is.
Murray River
Cohuna
Kow Swamp
Devil's Lair
Kaurna tribe
Narrinyeri tribe
VICTORIA
King George Sound
Devon Downs
Keilor
Melbourne
Port Phillip Bay
Gippsland
Kurnai tribe
Cave Bay Cave
Mt Cameron West
Flinders Is.
TASMANIA
Hobart
Tasman Peninsula

The Coming of the Aborigines

'The settlement of Australia began in 1788.' To most Australians this is a familiar statement, part of the story of their country's foundation and settlement. It has been white Australians who have put forward this idea—they have given the impression that Australia's history really begins at the time when white people first explored and settled this continent. Yet the truth of the matter is different, for Australian history goes back to other settlers. The first Australians were not white, but dark-skinned people, the ancestors of the present-day Australian Aborigines.

For many centuries the Aborigines were the only human occupiers of the land now known as Australia, apart from a few visiting Indonesian traders on the north-west coast. Almost certainly there was no attempt by other peoples to settle among them or displace them until Europeans began to do so late in the eighteenth century. While they were sole possessors of Australia, the Aborigines developed a highly organized pattern of living. They also developed, in the form of legends, their own stories of Australia's history which were passed down to their children. In these stories they explained the origins of their country and their own presence in it, trying to satisfy man's great curiosity about the past.

The Puzzle about Origins

What are the origins of the country and of Aboriginal life within it? If the first Aborigines did not originate in Australia, where did they come from? Why did they come? Did they come together as a single group, or in several groups over a period of time? How many came, and by what means? These are only a few of the questions that can be asked.

The Dreamtime

The Aborigines have found some of the answers to these questions in their stories of the 'Dreamtime', the period at the beginning of time when the earth was not formed as now but was more like a great plain stretching to the horizon. This was the creative period, when great spirit-heroes rose from the plain where they had been sleeping. Taking the form of animals such as the kangaroo, snake, or eaglehawk, they wandered the earth, behaving almost as humans, until

A canoe tree, Blanchetown, South Australia

this part of the Dreamtime suddenly came to an end. Some of the spirit-heroes went into the sky, and others into water-holes or the earth, leaving behind them signs of their earthly existence. These were in the form of caves, hills, rivers, holes in rocks and many other natural features in the landscape.

Yet the spirit-heroes did more than this. They left behind the spirits which were to bring about life in human, plant, or animal form, as well as laws, fire, and the first weapons and implements to help man live on the earth. All Aborigines and living things have thus been the descendants of these original beings, who themselves did not really die, but lived on in different forms. Nor in Aboriginal belief did the spirits of later Aborigines die—death is merely a physical end, so that a person's spirit survives. The past is thus linked vitally to the present and is very real.

The Aboriginal people have had a firm belief in the idea of the Dreamtime and its general pattern of creation. This idea has provided explanations of the past and formed a vital part of their religion, making clear the origins of living things, human and non-human. To non-Aborigines, who have different religious and cultural ideas, there are other ways of explaining these things.

Tracing the Past

It is not easy to offer a clear explanation of Aboriginal origins in Australia, apart from the Aborigines' own accounts. The passing of time has hidden evidence relating to the origins of the Aborigines and their movement to Australia. Early Aborigines left no written account of any such migration, and the seas now cover a good part of the land surface over which they would have moved to Australia. There are no written accounts in any other country about such migration, nor have Aborigines survived elsewhere.

Sufficient material evidence has been found at archaeological and other sites, however, to suggest the pattern of

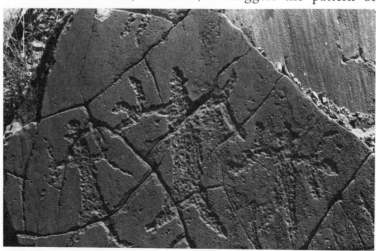

Disintegrating engravings of human figures on a rock face at Mootwingee, western New South Wales

Grooves cut into the walls of Koonalda
Cave, perhaps by Aboriginal flint miners

An archaeological digging site at
Fromm's Landing, River Murray, South
Australia

Aboriginal life before the arrival of European explorers and
settlers, and to offer explanations about the origin of the
Aborigines. Weapons and implements have been found in
considerable numbers, showing how Aborigines of earlier
times hunted and fought or performed the vital task of cutting things. Many material remains have been discovered at
former camp sites: stone tools, cooking hearths, anvil stones,
bones from animals, and shells from seafood. Scars on trees
reveal the source of materials for bark objects sometimes as
large as a canoe. Sacred objects have survived which tell of
the Aborigines' religious life and its importance. Examples
of old art remain, though some are now growing faint owing
to the actions of weather or vandals. Aboriginal art can take
many forms, and can still be seen most readily in engravings
or paintings made on a variety of materials. An interesting
example has survived in the Koonalda Cave on the Nullarbor
Plain, where an early sample of man's artistic efforts can be
seen in wall markings over 20,000 years old, somewhat similar to the markings left by prehistoric man in European
caves.

Much of what is known about former Aboriginal society
has come from studying these material remains. Australian
museums now contain large collections of them, helping
those who study the life of man to find out more about
Aboriginal society before white settlement in Australia. Yet
until fairly recently it was not possible to know with much

3

certainty how long the Aboriginal people have resided in Australia.

The Work of Archaeologists[1]

Archaeological research has helped to throw light on these problems. In other parts of the world such research has contributed greatly to man's rediscovery of the past, as in Turkey, where the diggings of Heinrich Schliemann revealed the ruins of the fabled city of Troy. In Australia archaeologists have not had the excitement of finding lost cities, but their work has had important results. In several places they have discovered traces of Aboriginal life in layers of debris materials, just as the archaeologists digging at Troy and at other famous sites found layer upon layer of the remains of older civilizations. One of the great pioneering efforts occurred in 1929, when N. B. Tindale and H. M. Hale excavated at Devon Downs, a site in a rock shelter in the cliffs along the lower Murray River in South Australia. They found twelve layers of remains, revealing at least three different cultural stages of Aboriginal life. This suggested that different migrations of Aborigines occurred in earlier times.

Since that time, and especially in the last two decades, archaeologists have made some very exciting discoveries in Australia. A number of these have been in caves. At Kenniff Cave in southern Queensland flake tools and stencil markings are signs of early Aboriginal occupation there. In Koonalda Cave in western South Australia Aborigines descended into

Ancient finger markings on the walls of Koonalda Cave (Scale in feet)

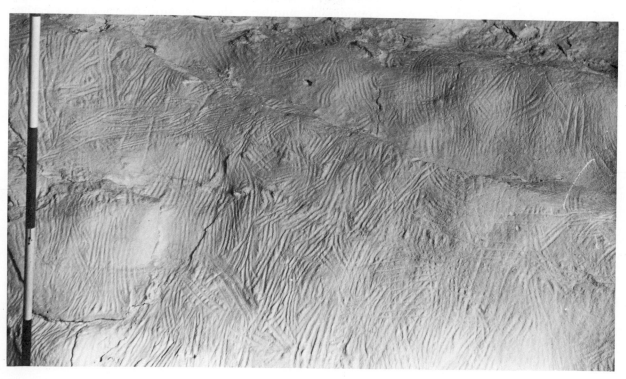

the dark cave perhaps to look for water and to seek hard flint for weapons and cutting tools. In the white walls of the cave there are curious finger-line markings, an example of the early art of the Aboriginal people. In Cave Bay Cave on Hunter Island, off the north-west corner of Tasmania, archaeologists have sunk trenches and found remains of native mammals, stone artefacts and charcoal. Other caves elsewhere have shown similar evidence of early human occupation. Some recently found caves in south-west Tasmania, on the Franklin and Gordon Rivers, reveal the camping-places of people who left behind great quantities of artefacts as well as the bones of animals they hunted.

Perhaps even more interesting discoveries about human life in ancient Australia have been made nearer the surface. In south-western New South Wales lies a series of dried-up lakes known as the Willandra Lakes. One of these is Lake Mungo, on the old shoreline of which have been found the remains of cooking hearths, animal bones and stone tools. This site, however, has provided something else—the skeletons of Aboriginal people who once lived there. One of these was a young woman, whose body was cremated and buried on the edge of the fresh-water lake. It seems, by the evidence of fossil remains nearby, that she and her companions hunted marsupials such as rat-kangaroos, native cats and larger animals. Other food included emu eggs, small birds, shell-fish and golden perch, a fish of considerable size. The presence of bone awls and other tools suggests that Aborigines there could have made skin cloaks to ward off the cold. Here, at an early time, a small group of Aboriginal people with a distinct culture must have established a camp for themselves. By deeper excavation, archaeologists have found stone tools which suggest that these people were not the first to live at that place.

Archaeologists rely heavily on different branches of science to help them investigate prehistory—the period before the written record. It was a geologist, Dr Jim Bowler, from the Australian National University who was able to recognize the fossil landscape of the Willandra Lakes and begin the exploration of Lake Mungo's mysteries. Anatomists have examined the human bones found, while other scientists have made careful investigations of further remains. A great problem, of course, is to decide the age of the material discovered. Excavations usually uncover progressively older remains as digging goes deeper. The bottom layers at any site may represent very old societies. But exactly how old? In the past this has been hard to tell, and it has been possible to make only general statements rather than accurate conclusions. Now, however, scientific techniques such as radio-carbon dating can give a more certain date to these remains.

Radio-carbon dating (Carbon 14 dating) is a technique developed after the discovery in 1947 of Carbon 14 in nature.

It measures the amount of radio-active carbon present in the remains of once-living animal or plant matter. Since such matter loses radio-carbon at a constant rate, it is possible to measure in a laboratory how long it is since the animal or plant died. This may give an approximate age not only of the animal or plant matter, but also of stone implements found in association with it. (It has been possible to check and improve the reliability of radio-carbon dating by comparison with tree-ring counts of bristlecone pine trees, American trees which allow a series of accurate counts to be made back for 7,000 years.)

In Australia the radio-carbon method has produced important results. It enables us to know fairly accurately how long ago Aboriginal people may have lived at or visited certain sites. Stone tools found in Kenniff Cave are about 19,000 years old, and a tooth found in excavations at Devil's Lair, at Augusta in Western Australia, is of a similar age. The Aboriginal markings in Koonalda Cave are about 24,000 years old. Human occupation in Tasmania has been dated to over 22,000 years ago at Cave Bay Cave, and to at least 19,000 years at the Franklin River. At Keilor near Melbourne stone flake tools have been found which are over 30,000 years old. The female Aboriginal whose skeleton was found at Lake Mungo was cremated 26,000 years ago, but a skeleton of a male Aboriginal found there in 1974 may be 32,000 years old. Indeed it now seems likely that humans may have been present in Australia for 40,000 years.

Theories about the Origins of the Aboriginal People

Radio-carbon dating may in future determine even older dates for human occupation in Australia. We know now, however, that at Lake Mungo in New South Wales, at Keilor in Victoria, and at Devil's Lair in Western Australia there are sites where people were living more than thirty thousand years ago. We can be less certain about where the Aborigines came from, and how and why their migrations occurred. Many theories have been put forward for an understanding of these things.

One early theory suggested that Aborigines did not migrate to Australia, but that mankind may have actually originated in the Australian region and that subsequent human groups evolved from there. This view was put forward in the 1920s, but has been discounted on several grounds, the main one being that fossil remains of ancient man found overseas, and his stone and bone implements, have been of an older period than similar remains found in Australia. Southern Africa is now believed to be the cradle of man. Man had moved from Africa probably along coastal routes to China and South-East Asia at least one and a half million years ago.

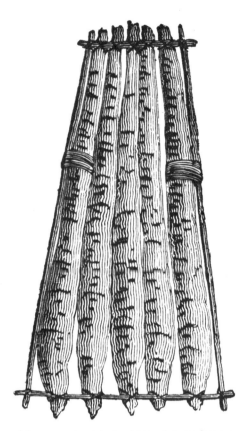

Mangrove logs lashed together to form a raft, Northern Australia

Other theories suppose that Aborigines may have come originally from Europe, possibly even being white at first and later mixing with dark-skinned peoples before reaching Australia. These theories, too, have been criticized, chiefly by those who believe that the Australian Aborigines originated in Asia.

The view that the Aborigines came from Asia is now widely accepted. There is considerable evidence for it. There are, for example, groups of people in Asia today who have physical resemblances to Aborigines and who may be part of the same original racial stock. The Veddahs in Ceylon and the Dravidians in Southern India are two such groups, while nearer to Australia there are the Sakai in northern Malaysia and groups in Indonesia, New Guinea and New Caledonia. These peoples have some physical and cultural similarities to the Aborigines. The Dravidians have also used the boomerang, and resemble Aborigines in other ways of living. Ancient fossil skulls found in India and Indonesia, such as the Wadjak skull found in Java late in the nineteenth century, resemble those of fossil skulls of Aborigines found at several places in Australia.

The Movement to Australia

Today newspapers in Australia have often reported the story of 'boat people' coming in refuge from Asia to Australia. Their arrival in quite small boats, hardly seaworthy for the lengthy journeys they have made on the open waters, seems strange and remarkable to modern Australians. And such journeys have stories of hardship and tragedy surrounding them, scarcely understood by modern Australians who travel in speed and style.

Man must have first come to Australia in such desperate manner, with much less chance of survival on the voyage and on arrival. We can only guess at why refuge was sought, and when the first arrivals occurred on part of what is now modern Australia. It seems certain that the earliest Aborig-

Aborigines on a log raft, Northern Australia

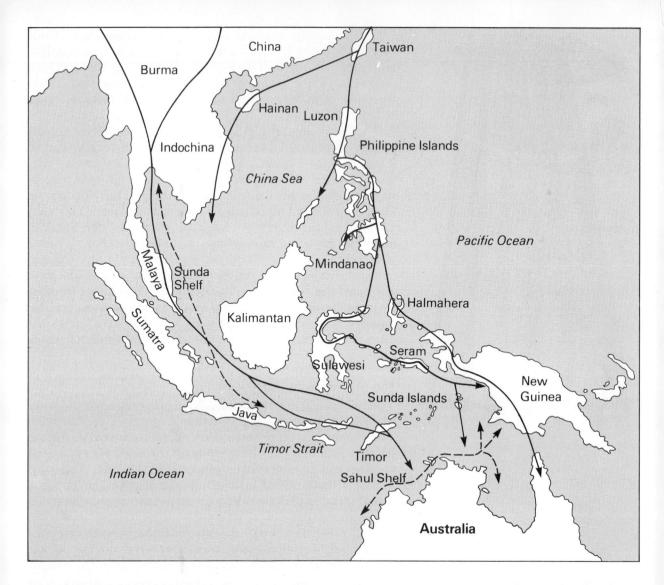

China

Taiwan

Burma

Hainan

Luzon

Indochina

Philippine Islands

China Sea

Pacific Ocean

Mindanao

Halmahera

Malaya

Sunda
Shelf

Kalimantan

Seram

Sumatra

Sulawesi

New
Guinea

Sunda Islands

Java

Timor Strait

Timor

Indian Ocean

Sahul Shelf

Australia

Possible migration routes to Australia in early times. Note the Sunda and Sahul Shelfs, which would have been exposed as land

ines had no large sea-going craft—probably they accomplished any necessary sea travel towards Australia by using the simplest methods of transport. Polynesians and Melanesians are known to have used canoes in moving from island to island. The first Aborigines may have used bark canoes or rafts made from poles lashed together—they have used both canoes and rafts in modern times.

It may seem that such craft would have been too frail for travel to Australia, but the Aborigines would have come at a time when geographic conditions in the Australian region were very different from those of today. In the Pleistocene period there were alternating periods of ice formation and warmer climate. During the ice periods (the glacial stages) some of the water of the ocean was taken up in ice. Ice sheets formed at the poles, and the lower ocean level caused land previously under the seas to be exposed. In warmer periods

(Above) An artist's impression of what a Diprotodon probably looked like, based on skeletal remains found in Australia, especially near Lake Callabonna

the ice melted and ocean levels rose, covering some of the exposed land. Aboriginal migration to Australia must have occurred when more land was exposed and shorter journeys by water were possible. In the last ice period enough water would have been stored as ice to expose now submerged land between Asia and Australia. The Sunda Shelf in South-East Asia and the Sahul Shelf to the north of Australia would have been exposed, establishing land bridges between former islands. Sixty metres of water now covers the Sahul Shelf, but in the last ice period New Guinea would have been connected to Australia, while to the south Kangaroo Island and Tasmania would have formed part of the same land mass. There would still have been water journeys from fifty to one hundred kilometres in length to make between Asia and Australia in such a time. How many people may have perished over the centuries in attempting those difficult sea crossings by canoe or raft? People were living in Timor 200,000 years ago—how much longer was it before they were able to reach Australia and ultimately survive as a race there?

The New Land

Man probably arrived in Australia in the Pleistocene period between 100,000 and 10,000 years ago, when the land was very different from now and certainly not unchanging. There were once glaciers on the Great Dividing Range and in Tasmania, and a higher rainfall fell across the country. Chains of lakes and rivers in now arid country were full of fish, and much vegetation clothed the land. Shell-fish were common. Man was not alone in this fertile landscape. He shared it with creatures of curious form, such as the Diprotodon, a shambling, four-legged creature with its big toes turned at right angles to the others. It was about three metres long, and resembled a hippopotamus; it was also the largest of the marsupials. There was a large kangaroo (Procoptodon) three metres high, which could pull down branches of trees, and a giant wombat (Phascolonus). Then there was the marsupial lion (Thylacoleo), with great slicing teeth and presumably capable of tearing the flesh of its victims. There were giant tortoises and koalas as well, while in places such as Lake Eyre there were once porpoises and crocodiles.

These creatures have died out from the interior of the country, and now remain as fascinating collections of bones and puzzles to science. Why did they die? What, for example caused the death of hundreds of Diprotodons at Lake Callabonna in South Australia, where they flayed about in the boggy lake in a last desperate bid for survival before the lake became their graveyard? Did Aborigines play a role in their extinction? Or was it climatic change that brought their end?

We know that Aborigines and the old fauna of the country existed at the same time. By the evidence of crushed and charred bones of the ancient animals, it is tempting to conclude that the arrival of man in Australia hastened the end of the animals. Rather than living in an easy balance with nature, man was an active agent in changing its appearance.

The most dynamic way in which man could have changed the landscape was by fire. The first European explorers by sea along Australia's coasts, such as Cook and Flinders, often noticed smoke and fires ashore. It is clear that Aborigines used fire extensively to burn the bush. Animals could be flushed out by this method and more easily killed. There was another effect—fire destroyed the existing surface matter and allowed new shrubs or green grass to grow. This practice has been called 'firestick farming', and must have been carried out for thousands of years. This can be detected by analysing pollen grain samples from cores taken at certain sites. We can thus have a tiny window into the past, and estimate by counting ancient pollen grains at different levels what vegetation existed in earlier times. Samples from cores taken from the floor of Lake George near Canberra show by the presence of charcoal that some time between 100,000 and 50,000 years ago there was a sudden expansion in the amount of fire in the land, and that the existing casuarina forest was destroyed and replaced by eucalypts and wattles. Were these changes brought about by Aboriginal man's arrival in Australia, and the beginning of the practice of firing the country? If that is the case, then the man-made periodic fires had a dramatic effect in changing the country. Its vegetation was altered, and other living things increased or decreased in turn. The Aborigines were able to encourage grass for game to feed on, or certain plants to grow which they could themselves use. This was not a practice carried on only in Australia, for other earlier peoples have used fire in hunting drives and as an aid to the growth of pasture. Like those peoples in other continents, the Aborigines were active in bringing about change in the world around them.

Other Ideas about Origins and Migration

In 1845 Edward John Eyre, the famous explorer and close student of Aboriginal life, made the following observation:

> The Aborigines of Australia...present a striking similarity to each other in physical appearance and structure; and also in their general character, habits, and pursuits. Any difference that is found to exist is only the consequence of local circumstances or influences, and such as might naturally be expected to be met with among a people spread over such an immense extent of country.[2]

From time to time prehistorians have suggested that while there may be a striking similarity among Aboriginal people in modern times, as Eyre observed, their origins go back to the arrival of different groups on the Australian continent. It is difference, rather than similarity, which has been the subject of investigation. Some years ago, for example, J. B. Birdsell suggested that there must have been three movements of Aboriginal people from Asia to Australia, and identified different Aboriginal people living along the Murray River, in Arnhem Land and in north-eastern Queensland. A more clearly marked difference was noted between Aborigines on the mainland and those in Tasmania. The Tasmanians, it has been argued, with their simpler style of living and their different appearance, could have come from Melanesia, drifting by raft or canoe in the Pacific and chancing upon Tasmania, as the Maoris must have come upon New Zealand.

In the last few years such views about the migration of Aborigines to Australia have been challenged by new discoveries and thought. Again it is difference which has been noticed, this time in the important fossil skulls which have been found in parts of Australia. One of the most significant groups of skulls has been those discovered at Kow Swamp in northern Victoria. They are from Aborigines who lived about 8,000—10,000 years ago, and had a more rugged appearance, with stronger jaws and flat receding forehead. At Talgai station in Queensland and at Mossgiel in New South Wales similar finds have been made. The Lake Mungo skeletons, much older, are those of a more finely-featured people, and more modern in appearance.

There are various theories about what these finds mean. Both types of remains are Aboriginal in form, but were there different groups who came to Australia in earlier times, or was there only one group, which developed in different ways in separate parts of Australia? It now seems likely that separate migrations did occur, and that the Kow Swamp Aborigines were descended from the first migrant people to come to Australia. These people, who may have come from South-East Asia up to 100,000 years ago, made the earliest ocean voyage known. They were followed from South-East Asia by a later group, of the modern type found at Lake Mungo. Some intermingling of the groups may have occurred in Australia, but in a few places the first people seem to have survived by themselves to as recently as 10,000 years ago.

Aboriginal man in early times may have retained a liking for coastal areas and remained skilled in adapting himself to the conditions there. The Lake Mungo people were living in a coastal manner on the edge of the lake more than 30,000 years ago. At other sites along the ancient coasts of the country, as at Devil's Lair in Western Australia and at Cave Bay Cave in Tasmania, there are further indications of coastal life more than 20,000 years ago. Probably some of the coastal camping-places are now submerged off the coast. Movement of the Aboriginal people from the north to occupy other parts of the continent may have taken place along the coasts and along the rivers.

The Tasmanians

The question of the origins of Aboriginal man in Australia has often been complicated by the puzzle about the early Tasmanian Aborigines. These people have become a puzzle partly because of their isolation for so long in Tasmania and because of their difference from Aborigines on the mainland. Few researchers would now be prepared to argue that the Tasmanians came by water travel from Melanesia. In modern times, for example, the Tasmanians possessed no craft capable of making any substantial water voyage. Nor is it now thought that the Tasmanians were the first arrivals in Australia and were gradually forced southwards by later migrants.

Tasmanian Aborigines and their canoes, near Schouten Island (A French engraving, published in 1807)

Hand axes used by Tasmanian Aborigines

12

The answer to the origins of man in Tasmania must relate to the oldest dates determined for occupation there and to the formation of Tasmania itself. At Cave Bay Cave man has been shown to have been present about 22,000 years ago. Just before this time Tasmania had been an island, with Bass Strait slightly lower than now, but as the world entered a colder phase ocean water was being taken up as ice, and Bass Strait became exposed land. It now became possible for Aborigines already in Australia to move by land to the south. This brought Aboriginal man to Tasmania, to places such as Cave Bay Cave. But at the end of the last ice age the waters rose once more, so that about 11,000 years ago Tasmania was becoming an island again. The land route to Tasmania was closed, isolating Aborigines there. The dingo, brought by man into Australia about 8,000 years ago, could not reach the island. Within it, the Tasmanians existed as nine tribes, speaking five languages. They kept to a simpler level of stone tool industry than Aborigines on the mainland, with apparently no ground-edge axes; they also had no boomerangs, spear-throwers or shields. They had a simple spear and clubs, and threw stones without the aid of a sling. Stone scrapers were their chief implements—they have been described as a 'race of scrapers'. It is chiefly deposits of stone fragments and heaps of shells that have survived to indicate their former life. They used neither nets nor fish-hooks, but left some fine examples of basketwork. There is also evidence that their culture may have actually become simpler over thousands of years. The Tasmanian Aborigines remained quite separated from any influence from mainland Aborigines.

Small scraping tools used by Tasmanian Aborigines

Woureddy, a Tasmanian Aborigine of the 1830s

Bessie Clark, one of the last of the Tasmanian Aborigines

(Below) Boulders engraved with designs by Tasmanian Aborigines, at Mount Cameron West, Tasmania

The Population

As the climate changed in the centuries after the Ice Age the Aboriginal people were concentrated in the more fertile parts along the coasts and adjacent to rivers such as the Murray, with the arid interior more sparsely settled. Aboriginal numbers in some parts of the interior had once been higher, as suggested by numerous large deposits of stone implements found there. Thus the Aboriginal population may not have been at its highest point when white settlement began in 1788. Aboriginal numbers in that year have been estimated at about 300,000, gathered into some five hundred tribes.

It may seem surprising that the total Aboriginal population at the time of white settlement was no higher than this. After all, it took only about sixty years for the white population in Australia to reach the same figure. Why were the Aborigines so few in number after so long in the continent? Undoubtedly the major reason for this was the unfavourable conditions over much of the continent. In drier areas, where food and water were often hard to obtain, a large population could not have survived. The effects of drought were a constant check on the Aboriginal population, depriving them of water supplies and of the animal and plant food necessary for existence. Even in the coastal areas which had a higher rainfall and a more reliable food supply Aboriginal numbers were often quite small. Major Mitchell, the explorer, gave a very low estimate of their numbers in eastern Australia, stating that there seemed to be only about 6,000 Aborigines in the area he explored, which was about one-seventh of the continent.

Other explorers and settlers recorded that the Aborigines were not numerous. Only a few thousand occupied a huge area of inland Australia, and only in present-day Queensland, where there once lived probably about a third of the total population, was there a large number of Aborigines.

The Isolation of the People

Aboriginal contact with the outside world must have been extremely limited once the continent assumed something like its present form. The only traceable contacts are those of Melanesian people from the Torres Strait and New Guinea region, whose influence has been noted on Cape York Peninsula, and of the Indonesian people who visited the northern shores of Australia. The latter were Bugis and Macassan seamen who visited Australia until earlier this century. Blown in their praus by the north-west monsoons, they managed to reach Australia at Arnhem Land, Groote Eylandt, and the north-western coast of Western Australia. There they gathered trepang and pearlshell until the south-easterlies came, whereupon they abandoned their coastal camps and began their voyage home.

The navigators Matthew Flinders and Phillip Parker King, while exploring Australia's north coast, met these seamen. King records that their provisions consisted chiefly of rice and coconuts, and that they carried their water in joints of

Macassan praus at Raffles Bay, Northern Territory, in 1839

bamboo. They had an important influence on the Aborigines, introducing into Arnhem Land iron for fish-hooks and for knives, and leaving traces of their contact in art and language. They introduced the dug-out canoe or *lippa-lippa* to the Aboriginal people there, who previously had used only bark canoes. It was also from these visitors that the practice of smoking was acquired—men, women, and children in Arnhem Land learned to smoke long wooden pipes passed from person to person. There was a significant effect of all this contact on the social and ceremonial life of the Aborigines in the area. Yet elsewhere such external contacts were unknown. The Aborigines remained the only occupiers of Australia, and for their part were apparently quite uninterested in exploring the seas around them.

Why did so few northern people in recent centuries make the journey southwards to visit Australia, and why did they avoid permanent settlement there? A white explorer acquainted with Australia's environment suggested an answer:

> …the force of nature was against it; the new land of the south held forth no inducements even for the pirate or marauder. In the hand to mouth struggle for existence, not even a supply of food would be found in a ransacked camp; no land seen tempting settlement by its luxuriant vegetation and produce. The visitors of the straits scorned the inhospitable coast, and returned north.[3]

It is important to find out more about early Aboriginal life in Australia. Not only can that tell us about the first Australians but it can reveal something of the way in which the human race spread and developed across the earth. As we learn more, nineteenth century views about the Aborigines as a very primitive people are becoming less and less believable, especially at a time when ideas about the theory of evolution are being questioned and modified. It is notable that Aborigines must have made the world's first ocean voy-

The Macassan trepanging settlement at Raffles Bay, 1839. Note the huts, cauldrons, and praus

Link With Early Man

Sydney—Skeletons resembling homo erectus —a species of man thought to have lived ½m. years ago—have been found in Victoria.

The bones are only about 9,000 years old, which has surprised anthropologists.

It means that a group of the species appears to have survived in Australia until comparatively recently.

Since the oldest known modern Aboriginal remains are between 25,000 and 32,000 years old, it also appears that two forms of men lived in Australia at the same time.

The discovery was made by Mr Alan Thorne, a research fellow in prehistory at the Australian National University....

Mr Thorne's discovery is by far the largest collection of remains found in Australia and among the best in the world.

The site is an old burial ground and the graves also contain stone artefacts, shells and ochre.

He has recovered more than 40 individuals and 'dozens' remain to be excavated.

Mr Thorne discovered the burial ground in 1968 after he had noticed the exceptional thickness of bones handed to the National Museum of Victoria by police.

They led to the anthropological 'gold mine' at Kow Swamp, near the Murray River, in Victoria.

Mr Thorne says the Kow Swamp skulls are exceptionally large and rugged and the face is like homo erectus, especially pithecanthropus from Java.

Radiocarbon dating has shown five specimens to be about 8,080, 9,260, 9,300, 9,590 and 10,070 years old.

Mr Thorne suggests his discovery indicates that at least two groups of people colonised Australia from Indonesia.

This extract from a newspaper report of 22 August 1972, shows something of the importance and excitement of archaeological research in Australia

age, that their art, especially with the frequent use of ochre, is extremely old, that their development of some stone tools and use of the boomerang were probably earlier than elsewhere in the world, and that their religious beliefs, as expressed through the Lake Mungo burial, are among the earliest recorded.

Undoubtedly further research will give greater understanding of this prehistory in Australia and its significance. At Roonka near Blanchetown in South Australia, for example, recent archaeological work has revealed burial remains spanning 18,000 years. The interpretation of the discoveries at this site alone may give much greater meaning and importance to the cultural practices of earlier Aboriginal people and the proper place of Aborigines in the story of the development of human society. This kind of archaeological work is at an important stage. As one of Australia's leading prehistorians has declared:

> It is my contention that on the stage of world prehistory, Aboriginal Australia plays a significant role.... Prehistorians are in a position to emphasize the dignity and individuality of the society which colonized the sixth continent, to document its diversity through time and across regions, and to preserve its monuments for posterity.[4]

1 For a detailed discussion of the material in this chapter, see the following books and articles, which have been found invaluable in the writing of this section: D. J. Mulvaney: *The Prehistory of Australia*, Penguin Books,

revised edn, 1975; J. Allen, J. Golson, R. Jones (eds), *Sunda and Sahul Prehistoric Studies in Southeast Asia, Melanesia and Australia*, Academic Press, London, 1977; 'Thirty Years for Thirty Thousand Plus'—An Interview with Professor John Mulvaney, *Hemisphere* Vol. 23, No. 6, Nov.–Dec. 1979; D. J. Mulvaney: 'Blood from Stones and Bones', *Search* Vol. 10, No. 6, June 1979; 'The extreme climatic place?', *Hemisphere*, Vol. 26, No. 1, July–Aug. 1981; 'From Earlier Fleets', *Hemisphere—An Aboriginal Anthology* 1978; and E. Stokes: 'Skeletons in the Sand' *Geo*, Vol. 3, No. 3, 1981. The radio cassette tapes 'Australia Before History', Australian Broadcasting Commission 1978 and Rhys Jones's A. N. U. Convocation Lectures 1979, 'The First Australians', have also been invaluable.

2 E. J. Eyre: *Journals of Expeditions of Discovery into Central Australia....*London, 1845, Vol. II, p. 206

3 E. Favenc: *The History of Australian Exploration from 1788 to 1888*, Sydney, 1888, p. 385

4 D. J. Mulvaney: 'Blood from Stones and Bones' (*loc. cit.*)

2

The Aborigines and their Material Culture

To the European discoverers of Australia and to the white settlers who followed them, the life of the Aborigines seemed to be primitive and harsh, lacking in comfort and refinement. This was not an unusual view, for Europeans have generally been very critical and intolerant of the pattern of living of native peoples in other lands. Yet in regard to the Aborigines, at least, Europeans have proved themselves hasty and unfair in their judgments, for the Aborigines had developed a society which was peaceful, well organized, and stable, and on a much higher level than commonly imagined.

It is important to examine what kind of life existed among the Aboriginal people before the effects of white settlement altered it profoundly. To do this it is necessary to rely on descriptions left by earlier observers and on the work of anthropologists and archaeologists. It is necessary, too, to note that not all aspects of traditional society have been destroyed, for there are still characteristics of traditional social and material life surviving strongly today, especially among Aborigines in northern parts of Australia. But because so much destruction of Aboriginal society has occurred and because white settlement brought about changes so quickly, it is necessary to look at the past, rather than the present, in order to get a clearer understanding of the Aboriginal pattern of living. This chapter and the one which follows are therefore written in the past tense, describing a society before some of its distinctive features began to change or be destroyed.

Physical Characteristics of the Aborigines

In many aspects of life the Aborigines showed how well they had adapted to conditions in the harsh Australian environment. As mentioned in Chapter One, there were some physical variations among them in different parts of the continent, which the environment itself or later migrations had brought about, but in general the Aborigines had similar physical characteristics. They had a brown skin pigment, usually darker in the northern part of the continent than in the south. Their hair was dark brown or black, though some children in the dry inland had fair hair which gained the typical colour only in adulthood.

The men often had fine beards, worn in various styles in

A man hunting in the Fraser Range, Western Australia, at the end of the 19th century

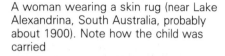

A woman wearing a skin rug (near Lake
Alexandrina, South Australia, probably
about 1900). Note how the child was
carried

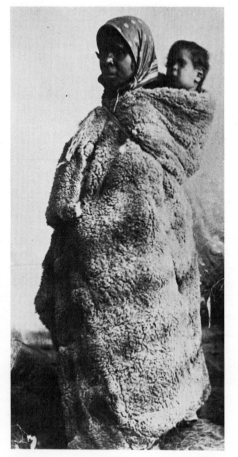

different parts of the land. (In the Cambridge Gulf district
of Western Australia they even treated their beards and
moustaches with beeswax, while in Central Australia the
occasional Aborigine who became bald would hide his
problem under a wig of emu feathers.)

The faces and heads of the Aboriginal people tended to be
long and narrow in shape, and their teeth were splendidly
formed and strong. They also had good eyesight, suffering
less from short-sightedness than Europeans, though their
keen perception of objects was more a result of knowing
what to look for than any exceptional physical advantage.
Thus an Aborigine would observe bubbles of air or pieces
of nibbled seaweed rising to the water's surface, indicating,
perhaps, a crocodile or dugong beneath. Eye disease,
however, was common among the Aborigines, in a land
where the effects of dust and flies were severe.

The physique of the Aborigines was well suited to the
strenuous life of hunting and food-gathering. Younger
Aboriginal people in particular were erect in posture, long-
limbed, and agile. One modern writer familiar with life in
the Northern Territory was greatly impressed by the grace
of movement of the Aborigines, and remarked:

> Have you ever seen the desert man on the move? Chest
> thrown out and head back, he does not appear to walk,
> but glides over the ground with springing stride; no fuss,
> no worry, the same pace, mile after mile, singing as he
> goes to make the distant object come nearer to him.[1]

This kind of graceful movement was not reserved only to
the menfolk. It was noticed as well in Aboriginal women,
who were able while on the march to carry water in bark
containers on their heads without spilling it, or piles of firewood in the same fashion.

The same easy and assured movement was displayed in
those other activities which made heavy physical demands,
such as stalking game, tree-climbing, or swimming. In tree-
climbing, for example, the Aborigine was expert, cutting
notches to assist his foothold, using a strong piece of vine or
rope, or merely pulling and levering himself up the butt with
hands and feet. (He also used the other method of reaching
the top of a tree—lighting a fire around the base of its trunk
and waiting until the flames had done their work in burning
it through.)

A man of the Milmenrura tribe, South Australia, in the 1840s, wearing a seaweed cloak

Adapting to the Climate

Part of the Aborigine's success in surviving in the Australian environment came from his ability to cope with extremes of temperature. In very hot weather the Aborigine took care to conserve his energy, travelling if necessary by night. A Central Australian Aborigine described how his people journeyed in such weather:

> …when aborigines are forced to travel in summer over long, dry stages, they do not set out on their journey until nightfall. Before leaving the last waterhole, they drink as much as possible, then keep going until a little after sunrise. When the day starts to warm up, the aborigines dig a hole under a tree until they reach the cool sand. Then they put a rough shelter over the top, reduce their skin temperature by throwing sand over their bodies, bury themselves up to the neck, and remain covered until the cool of the evening allows them to continue their way.[2]

In cold weather the Aborigine would sleep between fires at night, even if it meant sometimes suffering pain from rolling on to hot embers. The explorer Captain S. A. White recorded that the Aborigines used to laugh at the white man, who when camping made large fires that scorched one side of his body without warming the other. Captain White records that the Aborigines would 'sleep upon the ground in a row, hollowing out a place for their hips to rest in. A small fire is kept going on either side, and when it dies down the cold awakens them, and they put on fresh fuel. They do not really sleep for any time, just dozing off for a little while, and awaken with a start, in case the fires are out.'[3]

Generally the Aborigine preferred to live and sleep in the open, though on rainy or windy days he might construct a hut or windbreak, or if travelling carry burning sticks to provide warmth for his body. As an additional form of protection from the cold, he would smear grease over his skin. In some parts of the continent Aborigines wore rugs of possum or kangaroo skins to ward off the cold, but in general they adapted to the climate very well and did not seem to suffer unduly from their lack of clothing.

The huts of the Aborigines were known by a variety of names, such as *mia-mia, wiltja, wurley*, and *gunyah*, and were ideally suited to the needs of the people. They could be constructed in a very short time from materials near at hand, and were surprisingly strong and resistant to wind, rain, and dust. A small fire at the entrance provided warmth and acted as a deterrent to mosquitoes, while the dark interior discouraged flies. Bark, branches, and grass were the materials commonly used, the hut having a circular base, and a roof which was fastened at a peak or left rounded. In Arnhem Land Aborigines built a bark-covered platform beneath which a fire burned to ward off insects.

(Below) A wiltja in the Everard Range, South Australia, photographed on the Elder Expedition, 1891–2

A hut made from leaves of the fan palm, North Queensland

The Search for Water

A striking example of the Aborigine's ability to survive in a harsh land can been seen in the way he obtained water. In some areas, of course, water from rivers and streams was freely available, but in drier parts the Aborigine had to make an active search for it. In this search he showed exceptional skill. Water could be obtained from the roots and stems of trees such as the mallee, the mulga, the kurrajong, the needle-bush, and the desert oak. It might also be found stored in the hollow of a tree, notably the bottle-shaped baobab tree. The explorer David Lindsay saw an Aboriginal woman suck water from a cavity in a tree through tubes of bark. She had

Wailbri (Northern Territory) boys drinking from a rock-hole

found the water after noticing small ants rushing in and out of a hole in a fork of the tree. Often the Aborigine was guided to water by the presence of finches, pigeons, or parrots. He could also obtain water from rockholes and carefully concealed wells, which he often enlarged and the knowledge of which he might keep secret from other tribes. He also took care to cover the mouth of a well to prevent animals from drinking or fouling the water.

The explorers Ludwig Leichhardt and Ernest Giles found another means by which the Aborigines conserved water—the building of small dams, using wooden shovels. On occasions while travelling the Aborigines carried water in a skin bag or wooden vessel, or even, as in South Australia, in a human skull container, usually that of a deceased relative.

A skin for carrying water. These were made from possum, wallaby or kangaroo skin, with the fur turned inside and the holes tied

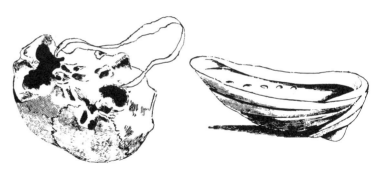

Drinking vessels—a skull with holes stopped up with gum, and a shell

23

The honey ant

Captain Sturt's description of drought in the interior of New South Wales in 1829

Often in dry areas they would simply rely on obtaining water from dew-laden grass, wiping or shaking the grass over a wooden vessel known as a *coolamon* or *pitchi*. A more unusual, but no less effective, method in these areas was to dig beneath the surface of a claypan and find a species of frog patiently awaiting the end of the drought. The frog had stored water in its body to tide it over such a period, and this water was perfectly fresh and drinkable.

No matter what method he used to obtain water, the Aborigine revealed his great knowledge of his country. He jealously guarded that knowledge. W. E. Harney, who knew the Aborigines well, records:

> There is nothing mysterious about it, just tradition handed on from mother to daughter and father to son, but with that tradition is a rigid law—none may disclose the secret watering-places of the tribe. To do so is to betray the people; therefore the native who divulges the secret is doomed to death. Observing this law they never camp near the water. No road leads to these places. Each person must take a different route and all tracks must be erased.[4]

To the Aborigines, living in a drought-prone continent, water was life.

There were a few other beverages, such as wild honey, available to the Aborigines. Sweet drinks could be made by soaking nectar-laden flowers in water, or by adding honey from the wild bee to water. It is said that in the north of the continent a drink was made by soaking the fruit of the pandanus palm. If this liquid became fermented, it produced a mildly intoxicating substance, drunk on festive occasions. In south-western Australia another drink, made by soaking grass-tree cones, had a similar effect. Water, however, remained the universal drink, and when drought pressed sorely and water was unobtainable there were scarcely any substitutes.

The Search for Food

The search for water was obviously highly important in Aboriginal life. Of equal importance was the search for food. Once again the Aborigines showed their great knowledge of conditions within tribal lands, their acute powers of observation, and their ingenuity in attaining their goal. Although there were considerable differences throughout the continent in the type and quantity of food available, the Aborigines became adept in hunting and food-gathering in their own local conditions. Along the coasts they became proficient in obtaining food from the sea. In the interior they were expert hunters of game. Where there were rivers and streams away from the coast, the arts of fishing were again found, while in hilly or mountainous country the Aborigine employed other skilful means of obtaining food.

A sea-shore encampment, Rapid Bay, South Australia, in the 1840s

These different food-gathering methods led to different forms of daily life. Hunters in the interior had to move about a great deal in the search for food in their arid surroundings; they had few possessions to burden them as they searched. Near the sea, however, it was possible to lead a much more stationary existence. Here the Aborigines had more equipment such as nets, fishing lines, and canoes. For the women-folk and children, however, methods of food-gathering did not vary so much—their task was to forage for such things as plant food, birds' eggs, small mammals, lizards, and edible grubs. Yet they were often more successful in finding food than the men, who might return empty-handed from a long day's hunting.

Food-gathering was generally a family affair, occupying a great deal of time and energy. It was an occupation in which young and old had to co-operate, especially since the Aborigines did not cultivate the soil. Yet despite what has often been said, the practice of storing food was not unknown among the Aborigines. In northern Queensland palm nuts and kernels were stored for months, and turtles' and birds' eggs were pulped and kept. In Central Australia Aborigines dried and preserved strips of kangaroo meat.[5]

Food from the Sea

At the coast the Aboriginal groups obtained a variety of sea-food, often enabling them to live better than Aborigines else-where. In shallow water fish were caught in traps or by driving them into hand-sewn nets. Other methods were to spear them from above or below the surface and to use a hook and line. Quite large fish were also caught—it was not

25

uncommon for Aborigines to feast upon mulloway, dolphin or shark, or even a stranded whale. In northern Australia canoes were often used to hunt fish. The Aborigines would throw harpoons attached to a long cord line, occasionally spearing a turtle or dugong by this method. If the desperate victim did not manage to break clear, the Aborigines would have secured a large amount of food.

The Aborigines on the North Queensland coast used a very remarkable method to obtain such a prize. A sucker fish, a species which fastens itself to a turtle or dugong by means of a disc above its head, was caught and then had a line fastened to it. Upon sighting their prey from a canoe, the Aborigines would cast the sucker fish towards it. After the sucker attached itself to the dugong or turtle, a tense struggle would begin, often ending with the animal being drawn near the canoe and harpooned. It was a task which demanded great skill. One observer declared:

> How they accomplish the feat of securing a turtle that may weigh a couple of hundredweight from a frail bark canoe, in which a white man can scarcely sit and preserve his balance, is astonishing. In a lively sea the blacks sit back, tilting up the stem to meet the coming wave, and then put their weight forward to ease it down, paddling, manoeuvring with the line and baling all the time. The mere paddling about in the canoe is a feat beyond the dexterity of an ordinary man.[6]

Other seafood obtained at the coast included crabs, crayfish, and many varieties of shell-fish. Along parts of the Australian coast great middens (mounds of shells) have been found, reminders of the Aborigines' liking for, and occa-

Fishing with nets in the sea, Rapid Bay, South Australia, in the 1840s

Fishing from a canoe, as depicted by an Aboriginal artist in the 19th century

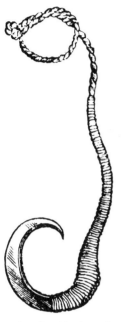

A fish-hook used at Rockingham Bay, Queensland (the hook is made from shell)

sional reliance on, this seafood. An observer records that a sand midden on the west coast of Tasmania bore abundant traces of the continuous feasting upon shell-fish, also of occasional banqueting upon the carcases of sea-leopards, seals, whales, and other marine creatures cast ashore.[7]

Food from Fresh Water

Middens have also been found along inland rivers. These rivers often provided a plentiful food supply, not only in the form of shell-fish but also waterfowl, fish, tortoise, and the platypus. The Aborigines paid careful attention to the weirs, nets, and traps which they set up in these waterways. The best known and largest of the fish traps were built on the Barwon River at Brewarrina in New South Wales. Here stone pens trapped fish when the river level was falling. The falling water level was helpful elsewhere, too—in Arnhem Land it allowed the Aborigine to spear the fine barramundi as billabongs dried up. Another method was simply to poison the water by soaking poisonous leaves, bark, or fruit in it, so that fish could be readily gathered.

The abundant food along the rivers allowed many Aborigines to live there. The lands along the River Murray were greatly favoured, as Captain Sturt found on his journey down that river. To many people, the Aborigines have usu-

A typical midden on Australia's southern coast

Women fishing for freshwater crayfish in the River Murray (Mid-19th century, S. T. Gill)

ally been thought of as essentially hunters of land animals— but one can also see how much food they secured from fresh water and from the sea.

Hunting Game

As a hunter on land the Aborigine was highly proficient. This kind of hunting was difficult, for native animals were wary and shy. In lean times it could take more than a day to track and kill a kangaroo or wallaby. It was vital to know the habits of the game being hunted, and vital to employ the arts of stealthy movement and patient observation. These skills have been well described by an early writer:

> As he walks through the bush, his step is light, elastic, and noiseless; every track on the earth catches his keen eye; a leaf or fragment of a stick turned, or a blade of grass recently bent by the tread of one of the lower animals, instantly arrests his attention; in fact, nothing escapes his quick and powerful sight on the ground, in the trees, or in the distance, which may supply him with a meal or warn him of danger.[8]

Camouflage and imitation were also used to aid the hunt. The Aborigine would carry or wear bushes, grass, and animal skins. His own body smell could be hidden by plastering his skin with mud. He would drag his spear between his toes and imitate the movements of animals as he followed his quarry. Other family members would often help in finding

Hunting emus (Mid-19th century, S. T. Gill)

A snare to catch small animals

Cord meshes of a kangaroo net

(Below) A hunting party (drawn by Yertabrida Solomon, an Aborigine from the Coorong, South Australia, 1876)

or surrounding the game, which was driven towards the spear-thrower or flushed out with fire. In the kill the Aborigine relied on a keen eye and a strong arm. The spear was the weapon most used, and it was thrown with great accuracy. The hunter could also bring down a bird with a quickly thrown club or stone.

Like fish, animals were often taken in nets placed along the paths they travelled. Another method was to dig a large pit on a path and conceal it beneath branches.

Animals such as wombats and echidnas had to be dug from their burrows, while tree-dwellers such as possums and flying foxes were pulled or smoked out of their hollows, or knocked from the tree by a boomerang. Water-fowl could be taken by an underwater swimmer breathing through a reed and pulling his victims under the surface. Major Mitchell, the explorer, witnessed another well-known method— frightening the birds into a net suspended across a waterway. Snares, nooses, decoys, and brush fences were further aids in the taking of game.

Wood grubs in a metal coolamon, Ernabella country, South Australia. Note how metal and other material has been adopted for use by Aborigines

Seeking Other Food

The search for other types of food was a less spectacular but nevertheless very important undertaking. Once again it demanded sharp eyes and patience. The womenfolk spent a great deal of time gathering the plant food, which varied in type. Generally it consisted of leaves, berries, roots, stems, nuts, and other parts of a number of trees, bushes, and smaller plants. The gathered food was prepared and eaten in different ways. Berries were eaten raw and seeds ground into a paste, while other foods were baked, pounded, or soaked. Soaking in water was commonly carried out to remove poisonous substances found in several native plants. In some areas where animal food was temporarily or permanently in short supply, as in Central Australia, plant food was greatly depended on. In the north of the continent there was often a greater variety of plant food than in the south, although foods such as yam tubers, which the women sought with their digging sticks, were found in colder as well as the more tropical areas.

Several varieties of insect life, such as white ants, larval grubs, and wasps, were also sought. One of the most desired was the wood grub, the finding of which demanded much resourcefulness, for these grubs lived in the roots of bushes or the trunks of trees and had to be detected by patient testing of the roots or by sharp observation of the bark. On occasion the sound of a grub inside the bark would indicate its presence. Once the grub was found it could be withdrawn from its hole by means of a hooked twig and then lightly cooked. Its flavour has been likened to that of a scrambled egg, slightly sweetened, or even butter. To the Aborigines wood grubs (in the interior often called witchetty grubs) were a highly desirable and important part of their diet, and provided good nourishment.

Sometimes the search for food produced other delicacies such as swan or emu eggs, freshwater crayfish, goannas, the honeycomb ('sugar bag') of the native bee, or the sweet substances produced by smaller insects. At times there might be a particular abundance of a certain type of food, and neighbouring groups would be invited to share in the harvest. In the south-east of Queensland, for example, the annual ripening of the cones of the Bunya Bunya pine was the occasion for many Aborigines to gather to feast on the seeds. Elsewhere a surplus of other food, brought on by seasonal conditions, could lead to similar gatherings.

Although there were many kinds of foods that the Aborigine might eat, there were some he would refuse to, because they were taboo. Tasmanian Aborigines, for example, would not eat fish other than shell-fish, and wallabies were taboo to many of them. In Gippsland uninitiated Aborigines were not allowed to eat female animals except for the wombat. Some foods were taboo to Aborigines for certain stages of their life or for the whole of it. In effect these taboos amounted to conservation laws which protected game which would otherwise be hunted. Even great hunger might not break these sacred restrictions on the Aborigine.

In all their food-gathering, the Aborigines gained from their great understanding of the environment. This helped them to survive quite well in areas where the white man would soon perish. This has been evident to many observers. Professor Abbie records:

> We have encountered Pintubi, members of a nomadic Western Desert tribe, immediately after they had completed a two-hundred-mile trek across apparently barren desert where the only possible food was little more than lizards and snakes. These people were hard, lean and fit and our studies of their blood showed no deficiencies whatever.[9]

Occasionally, however, conditions bore hard on the Aborigine. At these times hunger might force him to tighten the hair belt around his waist, and thirst might make him cover his stomach with earth. Extended droughts could even bring on death. It is a tribute to the Aborigine's abilities that such results were usually avoided.

Stimulants

In general the Aborigines were unacquainted with intoxicants, and used narcotic substances only to a limited degree. Apart from the habit of smoking introduced by the Macassans, the Aborigines chewed the dried and powdered leaves of the wild tobacco bush (*Nicotiana*), which contained very small amounts of nicotine. Another practice widely known

A wild tobacco bush, growing in the Birksgate Range, South Australia, near the Western Australian border

in Central Australia was the chewing of the stems and leaves of the *Duboisia* plant, known as *pituri*. This became a regular habit among men, women, and children, who liked the stimulating effect it produced.[10] *Pituri* also had another use: it was placed in water-holes from which an emu was likely to drink, causing the bird to become drunk and an easy prey to the Aboriginal hunter. The *pituri* was a small shrub and widely traded, as the following description reveals:

> The plant has the form of a small, stiff shrub with a number of straight stems, from four to six feet high, carrying yellow flowers and hard, narrow leaves. The leaves and little twigs are gathered…and packed tightly into bags made of woven fur-string.…These bags are traded for hundreds of miles, principally along an old trade route, passing from the north across the interior of Queensland and New South Wales, right to the south of Lake Eyre, shields, boomerangs, spears and other articles being traded back in return for them.[11]

Camps

The Aborigines were not solitary people. Gathered into tribes which in turn were made up of smaller sections, they were always conscious of belonging to a group. A portion

Flying foxes being placed in an earth oven and then covered with sand, Central Arnhem Land

Cooking a kangaroo in an earth oven

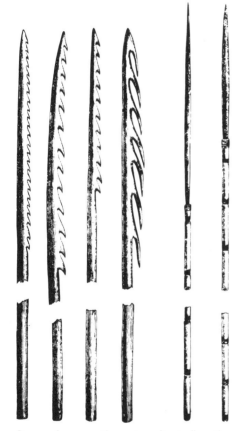

Spears from south-eastern Australia—the four on the left were used in fighting; the two on the right are reed spears, with a hardwood end fastened into a reed

of their daily life would often be spent in a group at a camp site. Some of these sites near available water were occupied fairly frequently. To such a place Aborigines would return after hunting, bringing food acquired during the day and sharing it among the group.

Valuable information about the daily life of the Aboriginal people has been gained by examining these old camp sites. In many of them blackened oven stones and fire stones have been found. Large animals such as kangaroos, wallabies, and emus were baked in ground ovens, which were hollowed out of the soil and into which hot stones were often placed to provide heat. Hot coals and ashes were used for the cooking of smaller animals, fish, lizards, and birds. A thick coating of mud might be smeared around a large bird, such as a black swan, before cooking. Of course there were different methods used among the tribes, but baking and roasting were always popular.

Some camps resembled small villages. Captain Sturt found a group of about seventy huts together on the bank of the Macquarie River in New South Wales, and J. T. Gellibrand reported a group of about a hundred at one place while on a trip to Port Phillip in 1836. At such camp sites material articles possessed by the Aborigines could be found. The largest of these articles would have been the canoes and rafts used by groups along the coast or rivers, or the animal and fish nets, often reaching to about a hundred metres in length.

Weapons and other Material Items

Anyone arriving at the camp site of an Aboriginal group, however, might have taken more immediate notice of the weapons to be found there. Prominent among these were the spears. These were mainly for hunting, though some had

33

A spear held in a throwing-stick, ready for throwing. Note the short hook, usually cut from or tied to the throwing-stick and fitting into the hollow end of the spear

ceremonial use. They varied in type and length—the longest being about four metres—and were tipped with hardwood, bone, or stone. A common spear among tribes along the River Murray was the reed spear, made by inserting a shaped and pointed piece of hardwood into a shaft of stout reed. To fasten the hardwood end, the Aborigines tied it with sinews from a kangaroo and completed the job with gum.

Many spears were thrown with a throwing-stick, often called a *wommera*. This implement, which had several other uses, gave greater leverage in throwing. Whether broad and bowl-shaped or narrow in design, it proved very effective. One early observer recorded:

> It enables a man to throw a spear with much force and great accuracy. Its simplicity and its perfect adaptation to the uses for which it is designed, strengthen one's belief in the natural genius of this people.[12]

An even better-known weapon was the boomerang, one type of which has become famous for its returning powers. Boomerangs were known among other peoples, in America, India, and Egypt, but the returning variety was invented by the Aborigines and used by them only. Boomerangs were patiently carved from pieces of curved hardwood, the returning boomerang then being given its distinctive lengthwise twist by heating and bending it. Returning boomerangs were used mostly in play, though they could be employed to scare birds into nets, perhaps along a river where the returning powers of the boomerang would ensure it did not fall into the water.

Non-returning or killing boomerangs were often larger and not so curved; they proved dangerous weapons, capable of inflicting severe injury when used in fighting. They had many other uses, such as for cutting meat, for stirring the fire when cooking, and for clearing the site for a camp. Not all tribes used the fighting boomerang—besides not being used in Tasmania, it was absent in some areas of northern Australia. Returning boomerangs had an even more restricted range.

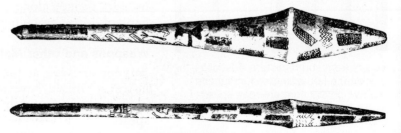

Clubs once used in Victoria

Another weapon was the club, often known as a *nulla nulla* or *waddy*. Like the boomerang it had a variety of shapes and decorations and was used in hunting as well as in fighting. To ward off such weapons the best defence was to use a shield or the base of the broad throwing-stick. The Aborigines in the central parts of Australia also used the shield to defend themselves in fights in which stone knives were used.

Stone, wood, and bone were materials widely used by the Aborigines. Stone implements, which can still be found at former Aboriginal camp sites, enabled the Aborigines to perform many tasks effectively. In areas where the fruits of the nardoo plant and grass seeds were crushed into a paste, grinding-stones were used to carry out the task. To beat out mallee bark into fibrous mats, Aboriginal women used stone pounders. To cut footholds when climbing trees, or the sheets of bark for a canoe, the Aborigines used an axe with a stone head. To carve sacred objects, to fashion spears, to cut meat, in fact to accomplish a host of cutting, carving, or scraping operations, the Aborigines used other stone implements, often finely shaped and of quite small size. The patience and skill they employed in making such objects can be

A fighting boomerang, a wommera, and a shield (rear and front view) from the Horn Expedition to Central Australia in the 1890s

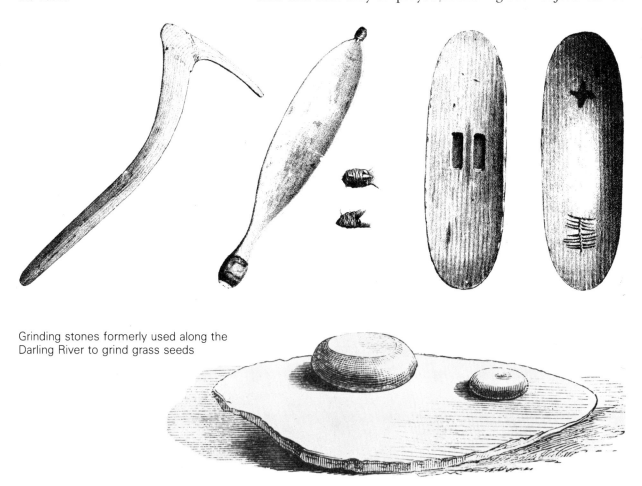

Grinding stones formerly used along the Darling River to grind grass seeds

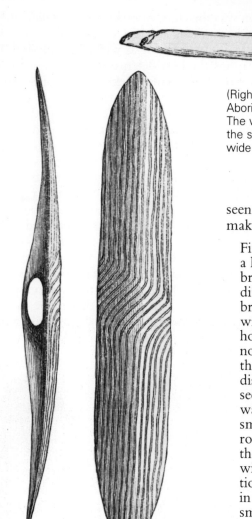

(Right) A stone axe, as used by Aborigines who lived near Melbourne. The wooden handle was 38 cm long, and the stone head 13 cm long and 5 cm wide

(Above) A Western Australian shield of the 19th century, about 84 cm long and 15 cm wide, used in combat in a half-kneeling or stooping position

seen in the following description of an Aranda tribesman making a stone axe:

First, a large, rounded, diorite pebble is taken; then with a lump of quartz the workman removes fairly large chips, bringing the stone down to something like the proposed dimensions. This done, a rounded pebble of quartzite is brought into requisition, and for a day or even two, he will sit, probably upon his heels, and patiently tap away, hour after hour, at the surface, taking off small flakes, until no sign of the original rough working is left. Then one of the nardoo mills, blocks of stone which are brought long distances, sometimes on the backs of women, for grinding seeds, is brought into use as a grindstone. With sand and water the axe is rubbed down until the surfaces are smooth; next comes the hafting; a withy is made and bent round the blunt portion of the stone till it holds it tightly; then the two halves of the withy are joined half-way down with two pieces of grass or other string. The next operation is to squeeze a lump of softened porcupine grass resin in between the haft and the stone; this done, a fire-stick smooths down the resin, and nothing more remains than to decorate the haft with red ochre.[13]

(*diorite*—a variety of stone; *hafting*—the fixing of the handle;
withy—a light, flexible wooden tie).

Wood had a similar importance to stone in Aboriginal life, and it had a wide range of uses. Log rafts, weapons, domestic utensils, sacred objects, and message sticks were some of the

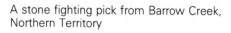

A stone fighting pick from Barrow Creek, Northern Territory

things made from wood. From bark came many other things, such as buckets in the Kimberleys, canoes, huts, sleeping mats, clothing, sandals, and wrapping material for carrying food or keeping a young baby warm. Shell, bone, gum, grass, palm-leaves, animal skins, and human hair were among other useful materials. The shell of an emu egg, for

Bone awls (top) for piercing holes in skins when making rugs, and bone spatulas (bottom) for smoothing seams

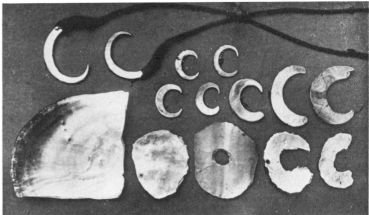

Pearl-shell fish-hooks from Queensland, showing various stages in making them

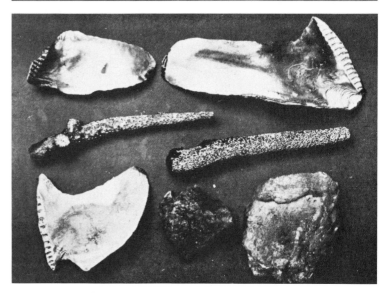

Queensland shell knives, coral files, and quartz implements

A wooden-hafted stone knife, made by the Warramunga tribe earlier this century

example, made a handy cup. Animal bone and tortoise-shell were ideal for awls or fish-hooks. Gum, obtained from spinifex and several varieties of trees, was of considerable importance as a cement. Kangaroo-grass was suitable for making nets, while water containers could be made from palm leaves or possum skins.

Trade

The practice of trade had an important place among the Aboriginal people. Through trade, local groups could obtain raw materials not found in their own territory and articles manufactured by skilled craftsmen elsewhere. Highly valued materials, such as ochre and *pituri*, were spread far and wide.[14] Stone for axe-heads was another important trading item. Tribes along Cooper Creek received stone from New South Wales, just as tribes in the south-east of South Australia did from Victoria. In some places groups of Aborigines opened up small quarries to obtain the stone, and met the demand from other groups not fortunate enough to have suitable stone on their lands. Some Aborigines made a name for themselves by their skilled craftsmanship in making implements. The Warramunga and Tjingilli peoples, for example, made knives which were eagerly sought among their neighbouring Central Australian tribes.

There was no particular form of currency used between Aboriginal traders, nor was trade confined to material objects. Ideas and rituals, such as art forms and corroborees, were exchanged as well. Nor was trade merely carried on over short distances, for trading routes spread across the continent, acting as great roads over which passed the valued objects and new practices. Aboriginal traders would sometimes travel hundreds of kilometres on trading journeys, bearing message-sticks or decorated spears to allow them to pass peacefully through other tribal lands. By means of such trade there could be found at many camp sites traces of contact between Aboriginal people and even with Indonesian people a great distance away.

Camp Life

One of the vital things in Aboriginal camp life was fire. To a white person its importance would seem to be in providing a source of heat, but to an Aborigine fire provided far more than this. By day, for example, it helped to drive out animals from their hiding-places; at nightfall it became the source of light. Fire was also used as part of the ordeals at initiation ceremonies. But fire had further importance:

> The [Aborigine] looks upon fire as one of the great indispensable quantities of his social existence; it is the element which dispels the evil spirits from his camp; it is the means by which comfort and friendship are made accessible to

Fire making by sawing hard wood across a softer piece of wood, and dropping dry grass on to the heated wood.

him; it is his universal companion. More than this, it is the fire, with its warmth and its light, which draws individuals, families, groups, and tribes together and through its agency and influence that social concourse is established which lies at the bottom of all conviviality, oracular discussion, and ceremony.[15]

The Aborigines had a number of explanations for the origins of fire. The Warramunga people believed two hawk ancestors first made fire by rubbing two sticks together. This of course is a legend passed down through the tribe, but it does actually suggest a common means by which Aborigines made fire. This was not an easy thing to do, and whites have merely achieved blistered hands in trying to copy the Aboriginal practice. The method was to rub a hardwood stick or boomerang vigorously across a piece of softwood, producing smouldering wood powder which was then placed on dry grass, leaves, or bark. This was blown until a flame resulted.

Another method, used more extensively, employed the same principle. The Aborigine used a stick as a drill, twirling its point rapidly in a slight depression in a second stick held firmly on the ground under his feet. Again smouldering wood powder was produced and used to ignite other material. A third method, adopted on a more limited scale in South Australia and western New South Wales, involved striking a piece of flint against a piece of ironstone. Sparks were given off which ignited dry tinder.

The men were responsible for making fire, and it was the men who carried the fire-making sticks when the camp was

Fire-making by the drilling method, as depicted in 1847

moved. Since all the methods of producing fire required some patience and effort, it was easier to ensure that it could be obtained from glowing fire-sticks brought from the former camp site. This was often the job of the women, who were also responsible for gathering firewood as well as carrying children, domestic articles, and water. The men would travel more lightly burdened, ready for hunting as they moved along.

Just as a camp was not complete without its fire, nor on the mainland was it complete without its dogs. These dogs were, of course, dingoes which had been tamed, usually from the puppy stage. With the arrival of white people in Australia new breeds of dogs were introduced, which interbred with those of the Aborigines. There was a great bond of affection between the Aborigine and his dogs. He treated them as members of his family, allowing them to share his fire and bed. They were not trained for hunting, but remained about the camp, eating scraps of food and giving companionship to the people there. The dogs also contributed to the noise of the camp, adding their yelping to the gossip of the women and the laughter of the children at play.

The Aboriginal camp site, however, was a place of activity as well as of noise. There the women, after carrying articles to the camp and helping to erect the family shelter, spent their time in caring for the children, preparing food, and making basket-ware and other articles. If food was

Striking stone flakes to make stone tools—a Wailbri man, Northern Territory

Wailbri men making stone axes

plentiful and there was no immediate need to hunt, the men also might remain at the camp site, engaged in making or repairing weapons and implements, cutting their hair, or just sleeping off the effects of a large meal. Such sleeping might seem a mark of laziness. Yet there was surely nothing lazy about a person who sometimes spent days tracking a single animal. Professor Elkin sums it up in another way:

> We have been told repeatedly that the Aborigine is lazy— lying about in his camp. Actually he is conserving or, rather, recovering his energy. We are apt to forget the powers of endurance the hunter needs in the long, relent- less chase after kangaroo, wallaby or emu; and the great patience, self-control and poise which he must cultivate and use....[16]

The Pattern of Aboriginal Life

The Aborigines lived according to a pattern quite different from that of many other societies. The idea of working for

41

Fishing from a bark canoe, with a small fire burning on wet weeds and sand. The firelight attracted the fish—a method often used along the Darling and Murray rivers

a certain number of hours each day and building up material possessions or money was foreign to them. The Aborigine took care to search for food before it was actually required, and was skilled in satisfying his material needs. What would have been the use of great numbers of material possessions? These would have been only a nuisance to the Aborigines, especially in desert areas, since they needed to move unencumbered in search of food.

After studying the Aborigine's ability to survive in the harsh Australian environment, his food-gathering activities, his material culture and something of his daily life, what general conclusions can be drawn? First, it is clear that the Aborigine had a vast knowledge and understanding of the land he lived in. He was able to exist quite well in areas in which white people, with different skills and equipment, still have difficulty in making a living. Although he did not construct great reservoirs, cultivate the soil, or rear animals, the Aborigine had an unrivalled knowledge of where and how to find food and water under natural conditions. He could read the signs of the bush with perfection. Every track on the ground was recognized and understood. Every seasonal change meant new things to find and hunt. Every watering-place on tribal land was known. It seemed that hardly anything in his environment evaded the Aborigine's observant eye.

In the second place, the Aborigine developed very effective means of supplying his material wants. In comparison to the white settlers in Australia his technology was extremely simple, yet he was able to perform a multitude of tasks by expert use of the materials available to him. Europeans thought that this simple technology was a mark of the Aborigine's backwardness. They tended to ignore the fact that it was a technology which had been developed to meet the needs of a way of life determined by the environment in which the Aborigine lived.

Europeans have looked down on the Aborigines, describing them as savages, ignorant and uncivilized, and lacking the intelligence of people in agricultural and industrial societies. This attitude has often been present in descriptions of Aboriginal people as 'stone age' and 'primitive'. Because the Aborigines did not have the same kind of material culture as Western societies it was believed they must be less intelligent. This belief is misguided in the extreme, revealing a deep ignorance of Aboriginal life and a lack of appreciation of the factors underlying the development of Aboriginal technology.

The Aborigines displayed the same genius for meeting their needs as men elsewhere. Difficulties were faced and overcome. Laughter and contentment, rather than dissatis-

(Below) A bark canoe under construction at the Murray River in 1862. The bark sheet, propped up at the edges and with stones and logs to weigh it in the middle, was heated by fire underneath and inside. The heated sap made the canoe soft and pliable until it dried in the shape required

An Arnhem Land bark basket

faction, were typical of Aboriginal life. Particular genius was shown in developing their social organization and systems of belief. These remarkable aspects of Aboriginal life, highly important though not easy to comprehend and interpret, are outlined in the next chapter.

1 W. E. Harney: *North of 23°,* Sydney, n.d., p. 67.
2 Described in C. P. Mountford : *Brown Men and Red Sand,* Melbourne, 1948, p. 59.
3 S. A. White : *In the Far North-West,* Adelaide, 1916, p. 82.
4 W. E. Harney : op. cit., p. 69.
5 F. D. McCarthy: *Australia's Aborigines—Their Life and Culture,* Melbourne, 1957, p. 60.
6 E. J. Banfield: *Confessions of a Beachcomber,* London, 1910, p. 245.
7 Robert W. Legge: *Tasmanian Aboriginal Middens of the West Coast,* in Report of the Nineteenth Meeting of the Australasian Association for the Advancement of Science, Hobart, 1929, p. 327.
8 R. Brough Smyth: *The Aborigines of Victoria...,*Melbourne, 1878, Vol.II, p. 248.
9 A. A. Abbie: op. cit., p. 83
10 A similar habit was known among native people in Chile and Peru, who chewed coca to invigorate ᐱthemselves on long foot journeys through desert.
11 Baldwin Spencer: *Wanderings in Wild Australia,* London, 1928, Vol. I, pp. 158–9.
12 R. Brough Smyth: op. cit., Vol. I, p. 310.
13 N. W. Thomas: *Natives of Australia,* London, 1906, pp. 48–9.
14 For the trade in *pituri,* see p. 26.
15 H. Basedow: *The Australian Aboriginal,* Adelaide, 1925, pp. 258–9.
16 A. P. Elkin: op. cit., p. 38.

Aboriginal Society

The previous chapter described ways in which the Aborigines satisfied their physical needs, developing a material culture which enabled them to live in often inhospitable parts of the Australian continent. They came to terms with their environment, learning how to obtain food, how to fashion implements, and how to perform many other daily tasks. It may seem that their obvious skill in providing for material wants was the major reason for their survival in Australia.

Yet there was far more to Aboriginal life than the ability to perform material tasks. It is clear that an important reason for survival lay in the carefully regulated social life of the Aboriginal people. White people have usually believed that Aboriginal society reflected a lack of refinement and 'civilized' practices, but once again this belief has been based on hasty judgement and a failure to understand the real nature of the Aboriginal world. Their society was far from being unrefined or barbaric—indeed, in its structure and organization it is considered by experts to be one of the most complex and sophisticated known to man. Each person had a clearly defined place within it. There were rules about whom he could marry, about his religious duties and with whom he could associate. Far from being a 'savage', the Aborigine was most careful in his personal relationships and in extending courtesies to others.

This chapter attempts to examine the social life of the Aboriginal people. Once again, it is best to look at it before the impact of white settlement brought so much change to the Aboriginal way of life. Of course, a number of the traditional social customs, obligations, and relationships described here in the past tense survive among Aborigines today, particularly in northern parts of the continent.

Childhood

The Aborigine's concern for others has always been shown very clearly in his attitude towards children. It is true that on some occasions the killing of babies (infanticide) was carried out, usually because of the effects of harsh seasons and lack of food, or because the baby was seriously deformed. The Aborigines, however, are noted for giving great attention to their children from the moment of birth to the time of their initiation into the secrets of the tribe. From birth the

An Aranda baby asleep in a *pitchi*

An Aboriginal child eating a wood grub—
a much favoured food—Musgrave
Ranges, South Australia

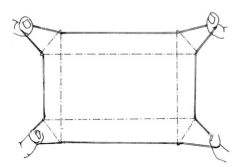

Diagrams showing steps in the making of a dugong design string figure, Northern Territory

Aboriginal baby was tenderly cared for, being carried in a sheet of bark or curved food-carrier. He was breast-fed for a considerable time, and brought up in close daily contact with adults and children in the camp, experiencing from his earliest days the company of others and the life of a group. Nevertheless he retained a strong bond to his parents, who took special care of him. They taught him his first words and his relationships to other people. An Aboriginal child also had a close relationship to his mother's brother or brothers. This person, the child's uncle, often acted as guardian of a boy child and was responsible for training him in the secret life of his people at initiation (discussed later) and on other occasions. The same person would often select a husband for a girl child, his niece. These relationships were of extreme importance and at the heart of the Aboriginal social system.

Aboriginal children in their early years were often allowed considerable freedom. Their parents spent a great deal of time playing with them and teaching them dances and songs. Many games were played. The boys took part in mock fights, throwing toy spears or balls of mud. There were games such as hand-ball, hide-and-seek, mud-sliding, and skipping. Children also played make-believe games or fashioned clever string figures from a length of vine cord.

There were in addition many practical activities to occupy their time. No chance was lost in explaining to them the arts of hunting. Children, especially boys, learned the calls and notes of animals and birds. They came to recognize the tracks of game, in fact so well that they could distinguish between particular animals of the same species. They even began to do some hunting for reptiles or birds and to help in the daily food-gathering.

An Aboriginal child learned by participating rather than by formal instruction. He grew aware of his place in the group and of the behaviour expected of him. After his early years had passed, he had to show greater obedience towards his parents. Children of both sexes would by this time have learned a number of songs and dances, preparing themselves for the more important learning of the ceremonial songs and dances of their later life. They would also have learned to bear pain, something which they might experience in ceremonies or on other occasions as they grew older.

For boys there came the time of preparation for initiation. At this time, between thirteen and sixteen years of age, they were removed from normal camp life, being separated from their parents, close relatives, and the women of the group. Girls, however, remained with their parents, until they were married. For both boys and girls the carefree days of childhood were drawing to an end.

Initiation

Undoubtedly the most important period for a young person was initiation. This took place at varying times among the tribes, but as a rule it was at the age of puberty. It was a period of great significance and ceremony, often lasting for many months. It marked the end of childhood and meant that a person was now ready to receive some of the sacred ideas and beliefs of his people. It was a time of testing and ordeal, preparing a person for the responsibilities of adult life and strengthening his physical and mental qualities.

It may seem that Aboriginal initiation ceremonies were devoted just to the physical marking of a young person. Yet to the Aborigines the physical part of initiation was merely the outward sign of something far more important—the recognition of the maturity of a person and, especially in the case of a young man, the passing on of some of the sacred ritual and secrets of his people. He was now at the beginning of his adult life. As time passed he would take part in further ceremonies, for he did not learn everything about the sacred life at initiation.

In a few tribes there was no physical operation at initiation. Where the operations did take place they usually consisted of circumcision, sub-incision, knocking out a tooth, and making scars on the body. Other practices included tossing the young man into the air several times or daubing him with blood. There was also ordeal by fire, a rite known in other parts of the world. During the initiation period religious beliefs and practices were revealed. For the first time the young men saw the *tjurunga,* symbols of the sacred life. They were shown sacred sites and instructed in mythology.

Thereafter the Aborigine entered more fully into the religious life of his people. As he grew older he took a greater part in ritual and ceremony, learning more and more about that secret world which meant so much to Aboriginal men and women. His greatest respect came to be for the elders, the old men who were the guardians of the wisdom passed down from generation to generation.

Marriage and Womanhood

Aboriginal marriages, unlike initiation ceremonies, took place with hardly any ceremony. At birth, or perhaps before, a girl often had a husband chosen for her, according to strict rules,[1] by a close male relative, or relatives. This arrangement was carefully respected by the families involved who, while the child was growing up, saw that certain duties were carried out and exchanged gifts. Often the marriage arrangement included the exchange of other sisters and nieces between the groups. The girl began to live in her husband's camp at the age of puberty. Since her husband could have more than one wife, the girl might have to share the camp with an older wife. To the Aborigines, a practical people, a new wife was valued for the help she could give in food-gathering and in carrying family belongings. Her life did not seem easy, and she might even suffer occasional physical

An Aranda woman and child

48

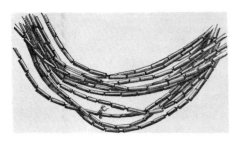

Part of a necklace of reeds (478 pieces in all), strung on twine and originally owned by a woman of the Burdekin area in Queensland

punishment from her husband, though she was capable of defending herself by well-chosen words or actually fighting back. She had to be a person of courage, enduring difficulties and physical pain with little complaint. Yet despite the gloomy picture often painted of it, an Aboriginal woman's life was not always harsh, nor was she a person whose nature became hardened by it. A modern anthropologist has said of her:

> Generally speaking she can be as kind and generous as any other woman: loving and fiercely defensive of her children, charitably tolerant of her husband and readily aroused to sympathy by the misfortune of others, especially children. The women love to chatter, gossip and joke among themselves, banter with the men and watch their children play. They enjoy adorning themselves... Above all they endure a harsh existence stoically....[2]

An Aboriginal marriage may seem to have been purely a matter of convenience. It is easy to criticize the apparent lack of affection between some husbands and their wives, and the wife-lending, polygamy, and jealousy that occurred from time to time. Yet such things are found in other societies, too—marriages among whites, for example, are not always noted for affection between husband and wife, nor for always being stable. As mentioned before, the Aborigines themselves were in fact most careful about their personal relationships. Their society consisted of a number of different social groups in which the position of each person was carefully established. Non-Aborigines have usually misunderstood this system; those who have tried to understand it in detail have noted how complicated the system can be, but how carefully and how well it controls social life.

The Tribe

The best-known unit of Aboriginal society has been the tribe. The first European settlers in Australia frequently used the term 'tribe' when describing the Aborigines, and referred to 'chiefs' leading the tribes. No doubt they were comparing the Aborigines to the American Indians or people in the Pacific islands. The Aborigines, though, had no chiefs of this type, and the tribe itself was not really as important a unit as often thought. All the members of a tribe, for example, seldom met together, if at all. There was no central governing body which organized the affairs of the tribe, nor did it work as a single economic body. Clans and the small local groups were of much greater importance in Aboriginal society, and the tribe was thus not the most vital unit to which the Aborigines felt they belonged.

What, then, was an Aboriginal tribe? It was a collection of people, numbering from about a hundred to as many as

49

The contents of a native woman's bag are:—A flat stone to pound roots with; earth to mix with the pounded roots; quartz, for the purpose of making spears and knives; stones for hatchets; prepared cakes of gum, to make and mend weapons, and implements; kangaroo sinews to make spears and to sew with; needles made of the shin bones of kangaroos, with which they sew their cloaks, bags, &c.; opossum hair to be spun into waist belts; shavings of kangaroo skins to polish spears, &c.; the shell of a species of mussel to cut hair, &c. with; native knives; a native hatchet; pipe clay; red ochre, or burnt clay; yellow ochre; a piece of paper bark to carry water in; waistbands, and spare ornaments; pieces of quartz, which the native doctors have extracted from their patients, and thus cured them from diseases; these they preserve as carefully as Europeans do relics. Banksia cones (small ones), or pieces of a dry white species of fungus, to kindle fire with rapidity, and to convey it from place to place; grease, if they can procure it from a whale, or from any other source; the spare weapons of their husbands, or the pieces of wood from which these are to be manufactured; the roots, &c. which they have collected during the day. Skins not yet prepared for cloaks are generally carried between the bag and the back, so as to form a sort of cushion for the bag to rest on.

Contents of an Aboriginal woman's bag, suggesting some activities in daily life (From G. Grey: *Journals of Two Expeditions of Discovery*, London, 1841, Vol. II p. 266)

fifteen hundred, speaking a common language and sharing similar customs and beliefs. It occupied a recognized area of land, and all tribal members living within it believed themselves to be related. Sometimes the differences between tribes were a little blurred, so that a common name could be given to a group of tribes (such as the Narrinyeri on the south coast of South Australia), but normally there seemed to be no strong ties between tribes. The tribe was a loose-knit body, which in more extreme cases, such as the Aranda in Central Australia, appeared to be in process of breaking up into sub-tribes or new tribes.

It is important to note that each tribe had its own territory, but that this territory was not just a place for obtaining food and carrying out normal daily tasks. The Aborigines regarded the tribal territory as their spirit-home in which their ancestors and tribal heroes had lived, and still lived. Thus they were bound to their land by strong ties of mythology, and would not leave it. When an Aborigine referred to 'my country' he meant not just the area where he hunted but the home of his ancestral spirits. Within the tribal boundaries were many sacred sites, which made the land of far greater importance than just for hunting and food-gathering.

The Local Group, the Family, and Kinship

As mentioned, the tribe was a less important unit than the local group. This was composed of closely related families who lived together from day to day, hunting and food-gathering over their own area of land, to which they also had close spiritual ties. The group's members worked together, not just for themselves. Food was shared according to strict rules, so that the old as well as the young were provided for. The families within such a group often acted by themselves, and were the basic units of it; they were related to other families in the group through the father, so that the group was formed around close male relatives of different generations. Sons born to members of the group would stay in it all their lives, but normally could not marry a girl within it. Daughters would leave the group when joining their husbands, but remain members of the clan which had spirit-homes in the old locality.

In Aboriginal society the basic family unit—a man, his wife or wives, and their children—was very important. Strong bonds existed between its members and members of the local group. In fact the bonds went further, for the Aboriginal people of a tribe, and even beyond it, regarded themselves as linked together in groups of relatives. Behind this idea were the beliefs of kinship, which varied in some places and can be very difficult to understand. Basically, kinship rules considered some of the relatives of the same gen-

The above diagram shows how an Aboriginal boy, in a family of three children would classify some of his nearest relatives. Note how under this system he would have another father, mother, brother and sister instead of another uncle, aunt and cousins.

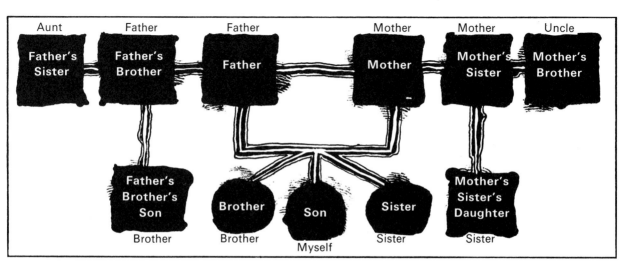

| Aunt | Father | Father | | Mother | Mother | Uncle |

Father's Sister — Father's Brother — Father — Mother — Mother's Sister — Mother's Brother

Father's Brother's Son (Brother) — Brother (Brother) — Son (Myself) — Sister (Sister) — Mother's Sister's Daughter (Sister)

eration as equal, so that to an Aborigine his father's brothers were all regarded as 'fathers', not uncles, while their male children were regarded as 'brothers', not cousins. On his mother's side, her sisters were regarded as 'mothers', and their daughters as 'sisters'. (On the other hand, father's sisters and mother's brothers were regarded as aunts and uncles.) An Aborigine thus grouped a number of relatives under a similar name. Kinship groups were recognized within each tribe, and each 'skin group', as it was sometimes known, had its own name and customs. Marriages were arranged to members of other kinship groups, often between people recognized as cousins. Great care was taken to see that incest was avoided.

These ideas of kinship and of other groupings such as moieties and clans within Aboriginal society remain complicated, and little detail about them can be given here. The important point is that social relationships and patterns of behaviour towards other people were clearly determined by the kinship system. There were rules governing many different kinds of action, besides the choosing of a marriage partner. By these rules a man was forced to avoid contact with certain people, such as his mother-in-law, or directed to perform religious and other duties, or guided in the proper sharing of food. In this well-ordered society rules had to be respected, for the good of all. If they were broken, punishment followed, which in extreme cases might be death. Punishment was on the eye-for-eye, tooth-for-tooth principle, and disagreements were often settled by duelling with spears, clubs, or digging-sticks. Settling such things was carried out as soon as possible, so that the peaceful pattern of group life could be restored.

The Elders

In all aspects of Aboriginal life great respect was shown for the elders, whose grey hair usually marked them out from others. It was not always old age that distinguished them, however; they were still active men whose years had given them greater experience in practical affairs and a fuller knowledge of the sacred life of their people. These elders acted as a council, and made decisions affecting group mem-

An Aboriginal drawing in the 19th century, showing what might happen in a duel

Elaborate ground designs representing
the travels of the great culture heroes of
New South Wales and Victoria

bers. They might, for example, settle an argument or decide a course of action to be followed. Perhaps one of them would be particularly important and his advice thus specially heeded, although he was not a king or chief.

The Spiritual Life

Throughout all these social arrangements there was a very strong thread of religious feeling, so strong in fact that it is impossible to understand the Aboriginal manner of living without being aware of it. This can be seen again in the relationship of the Aborigines to the land. Individuals did not own land in the European sense—the land they occupied was passed down from previous generations and entrusted to them. It has been said that the land seemed to own *them*, rather than the reverse, since it was the spiritual home of their ancestors, who included the ancestral beings who had wandered the land in the Dreamtime. Therefore the Aborigines regarded this land, and the parts of it occupied by local groups, as entrusted to their care, rather than owned for a practical purpose. The clans (groups of people related by descent from a common ancestor) would jealously guard their spirit-homes, including the sacred sites of their clan and sacred rituals, totems, and songs. They regarded the land in a religious as well as a practical way, as a home of the ancestral spirits as well as a source of food and materials.

It is clear that the Aborigine was a very religious person whose life was strongly shaped by his beliefs. The anthropologist F. D. McCarthy has summarized this well:

> To the initiated man his religion explains the origin of life itself and of his tribal customs, the source of his supply of food and raw materials, and the mysterious world beyond the comprehension of his scientific or general knowledge. To him it is a religion of great sanctity, inspiring in its mythology and songs, and impressive in its often colourful ceremonies. . . . It becomes a most important part of the adult life of the men, demanding a great deal of time and energy in the enactment of ritual, a tremendous concentration of intelligence in the memorization of the myths, song-cycles, ritual procedure and art designs, and an absolute faith in the efficacy of the beliefs and ceremonial activities.[3]

At the heart of Aboriginal religion was the idea of the Dreamtime, outlined in Chapter One. This idea was kept alive in the stories of the ancestral spirits, stories which varied among the tribes but were usually rich in detail. These are often referred to as myths, though to the Aborigines they were not myths but truths which formed the basis of their social living. The sky-heroes laid down the patterns of behaviour which had to be followed—failure to observe these and failure to carry out rituals correctly could result in lack of rain or food, and punishment for the wrong-doer.

HOW THE SUN WAS MADE

For a long time there was no sun only a moon and stars. That was before there were men on the earth, only birds and beasts, all of which were many sizes larger than they are now.

One day, Dinewan, the emu, and Brälgah, the native companion, were on a large plain near the Murrumbidgee. There they were quarrelling and fighting. Brälgah, in her rage, rushed to the nest of Dinewan, seized from it one of the huge eggs in it, which she threw with all her force up to the sky. There it broke on a heap of firewood, which burst into a flame as the yellow yolk spilt all over it, which flame lit up the world below, to the astonishment of everything on it. They had only been used to the semi-darkness, and were dazzled by such brightness.

A good spirit who lived in the sky saw how bright and beautiful the earth looked when lit up by this blaze. He thought it would be a good thing to make a fire every day, which from that time he has done. All night he and his attendant spirits collect wood, and heap it up. When the heap is nearly big enough they send out the morning star to warn those on earth that the fire will soon be lit.

They, however, found this warning was not sufficient, for those who slept saw it not. Then they thought they must have some noise made at dawn of day to herald the coming of the sun and waken the sleepers. But they could not decide upon to whom should be given this office for a long time.

At last one evening they heard the laughter of Gougourgahgah, the laughing jackass, ringing through the air. 'That
is the noise we want,' they said. Then they told Gougourgahgah that as the morning star faded and the day dawned he
was every morning to laugh his loudest, that his laughter
might awaken all sleepers before sunrise. If he would not agree
to do this then no more would they light the sun-fire, but let
the earth be ever in twilight again.

But Gougourgahgah saved the light for the world, and
agreed to laugh his loudest at every dawn of day, which he
has done ever since, making the air ring with his loud cackling
'gou-gour-gah-gah, gou-gour-gah-gah, gou-gour-gah-gah'.

When the spirits first light the fire it does not throw out
much heat. But in the middle of the day when the whole heap
of firewood is in a blaze, the heat is fierce. After that it begins
to die gradually away until only the red coals are left at sunset,
and they quickly die out, except a few the spirits cover up with
clouds, and save to light the heap of wood they get ready for
the next day.

Children are not allowed to imitate the laughter of Gougourgahgah, lest he should hear them and cease his morning
cry. If children do laugh as he does, an extra tooth grows above
their eye-tooth, so that they carry a mark of their mockery in
punishment for it, for well do the good spirits know that if
ever a time comes wherein the Gougourgahgahs cease laughing
to herald the sun, then the time will have come when no more
Daens are seen in the land, and darkness will reign once more.

A tree-carving of Biami

A stone arrangement on a ceremonial ground at Woomera, South Australia. This extensive stone arrangement was formed by clearing gibbers and making an irregular outline with stones

The great stories were passed down through the centuries and became the subjects of important rituals among the Aboriginal people. Sometimes they told of the doings of an honoured sky-hero, who was known by various names, such as *Biami* in parts of New South Wales, *Bunjil* in central and western Victoria, and *Biamban, Goin,* and *Nurelli* elsewhere. Along the lower Murray there was the belief in the Rainbow-Serpent, who appearing as a rainbow in the sky at the time of rain was naturally regarded as the maker of rain and the cause of the rejuvenation of the land. Another great ancestral being was the Earth Mother, who the Aborigines believed came from the islands to the north of Australia. She left her spirit-children who were the ancestors of different tribes. Great rituals developed about this idea, such as the *Kunapipi* ceremonies in northern Australia. In these ceremonies, held in the dry season, ideas of rebirth and fertility were stressed. These rituals spread to other tribes, and were carried out with much reverence

Of course, it was the fully initiated men, and especially the elders, who were the guardians of these traditional cults and who were responsible for passing them on to the next generation. They had the greatest knowledge of them and determined when the appropriate rituals were to be held. The rituals were dramatic performances in which acting, singing, and dancing were very important. The parts had to be learned by heart, and the whole performance had greater significance because the actors seemed to become the ancestral beings themselves. The ceremonies were held on sacred ground; usually they could not be seen by the uninitiated or

Ayers Rock, Northern Territory, an important totemic site—a photo taken about 1900. 'Every precipice, cave, gutter, and mark on the top and sides of the Rock commemorates the exploits and adventures of the creatures of…long-distant times.'—C. P. Mountford

members of the female sex. As part of the ritual, designs of great totemic significance were painted on the bodies of the participants, on the ground, on rock surfaces, or on sacred objects. For this purpose the Aborigines used ochre, human blood, and birds' down. A head-dress of grass, twigs, and human hair might complete the decoration.

The whole effect of the material decoration was very colourful, but there were other objects which gave vital meaning to the sacred ceremonies. These were the visual representations of the sacred life, usually known by the name *tjurunga* or *churinga*. Natural features such as trees, hills, or groups of boulders frequently had sacred significance, but the term *tjurunga* has normally been applied to smaller portable objects of wood or stone. They were usually flat and oval-shaped, with tracks and designs of circles, dots, and curved lines cut into them, The *tjurunga* were jealously guarded, since they were of the highest importance in initiation, fertility, and Dreamtime ceremonies and were held to possess great power. Personal *tjurunga* gave strength to the initiated men who owned them, and on occasions were lent as signs of strong friendship. Other *tjurunga*, such as the larger sacred boards or poles, belonged to a group. There was also the bull-roarer, a small slab of flattened wood which was whirled on the end of a piece of string; the resulting sound warned the uninitiated away from sacred ceremonies.

The Natural World and Totemism

The Aboriginal people clearly lived very close to nature, or more correctly, regarded themselves as at one with nature. They saw themselves as part of a natural order in which animals, plants, and the Aborigines themselves were linked together. The heavens, too, were part of this natural order. The sky seemed always close, in fact only a little higher than the highest tree; it was the home of the heroes who after their earthly deeds perhaps lived on as stars. The Milky Way was a path over which the sky-people travelled, while the Sun-woman with her fiery torch and the Moon-man with his smaller torch gave light to all the world. The Aurora Australis was the blood shed by men fighting a great battle, and a shooting star was a medicine-man's firestick dropped to kill someone. Explanations might vary, but there was little that seemed strange and impossible to understand in the heavens or on the earth. Man's task was to learn to live in harmony with the many living things that shared the world with him.

This task was made easier for the Aborigines by their idea of totemism. For the Aborigines totemism brought man and his environment together. It was not an idea known only to the Aborigines; people such as the American Indians held a similar idea. In Aboriginal society individuals had their own totem, which identified them with a natural object. The members of the bandicoot totemic group, for example, believed in their special link with that animal, which as their totem became their guardian. Yet the bandicoot was more than this, for it became the symbol of the common ancestry of members of the group, linking them to the Dreamtime and its heroes. Each Aboriginal clan had its totem and, since the clan could also include plants and animals, a special relationship existed between its human and non-human members.

As in other matters there were differences in the way totemism was observed. In some parts a person's totem was identified by the elders, who decided exactly what spirit-child could have entered a mother's body through a partic-

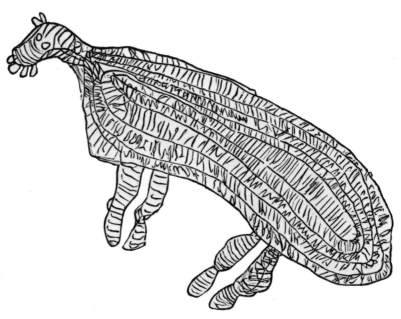

A bunyip, drawn by a River Murray Aborigine in 1848. The bunyip was much dreaded, and believed to live in a deep water-hole or swamp

ular food she had eaten, or through her being near a totem centre at some stage. Some types of totem were inherited—a child could inherit the totem of his father's cult group or of his maternal uncle. But everywhere the totems were greatly honoured, and no one could normally kill or eat his personal totem animal or plant; on the contrary, he would carry out rituals to increase its numbers. Thus totems were held in great respect, having a religious significance to the Aborigine. The athropologist Herbert Basedow gave an instance of this:

> I well remember on one occasion on the Alberga River I discovered a small black and yellow banded snake which I killed. An Aluridja man who was attached to the party at the time was greatly shocked at this, and, with genuine sorrow, told me that I had killed his 'brother'. Turning to an Arunndta he lamented aloud: *'Kornye! Nanni kallye nuka kalla illum,'* which literally translated means: 'Oh dear! This brother of mine is dead.'[4]

Death

Totems played a vital part in Aboriginal life, emphasizing how close the Aborigines were to the spirit-world around them. They believed that the world abounded with spirits, some friendly, some hostile. This belief supplied the Aborigines with explanations about the origin of human life, and

A 19th century illustration of huts erected over the graves of dead persons, next to the River Murray. The huts helped to ward off dingoes

also helped to explain what happened at death. Death always marked the end of physical life only, for the spirit of the dead person was released from the body and did not die. It would make its way to a home in the sky with the sky-heroes, or to a spirit-centre such as a water-hole. In some tribes it was believed that the spirit was carried across the sea to a land of the dead. Perhaps at some future time the spirit would be re-born in human form again and live another earthly existence.

The whole matter of what happened after death can be complicated, for the Aborigines often believed that there was another form of the dead man's spirit which has been called the 'trickster spirit'. The trickster spirit was a mischievous thing, for it sought to remain near the dead person and cause trouble. It was best not to disturb it. After mourning their loss, often with loud wailing and gashing of their bodies, the members of the family left the scene of death. To prevent any further chance of arousing the trickster spirit, the use of the dead person's name was avoided. The reminders of death were visible ones, such as a mound grave or a platform on which the body was placed in a tree, or the white clay and bark armlets marking those who mourned.

A woman ornamented with clay as a sign of mourning

A noose used for strangling an enemy

Magic, Sorcery, and Medicine-Men

The death of a person not grown old, nor killed in fighting, was said to be due to the work of an enemy. This touches closely on the matter of magic, a powerful factor in Aboriginal life. The Aborigines believed that death could be brought about by the magic practised by another person. A death so caused had to be avenged, and every attempt was made to find a person who might have been responsible. This could have been someone who had quarrelled with the dead person or shown jealousy, or who had offended in some other way. A number of signs might identify the guilty person, and to settle the matter a revenge expedition might be sent or an agreement worked out with the guilty party.

Pointing a bone, a symbolic way of spearing a person, was one method of causing death by magical power. It was carried out by a sorcerer, who pointed the bone towards his intended victim while 'singing' his death by ritual chanting. Death could also be brought about by performing ritual magic on the property of a person, or on a grass or bark likeness of him. In Central Australia there was the *kurdaitja* tradition—a party of *kurdaitja* men wearing shoes made of emu feathers worked their deadly powers against a victim. Sorcery, however, was not a day-to-day practice, for in fact there were few sorcerers among the tribes—but no one doubted its power. An Aborigine who knew he had been subjected to a sorcerer's work would invariably die unless stronger counter-magic, such as the securing of the pointing-

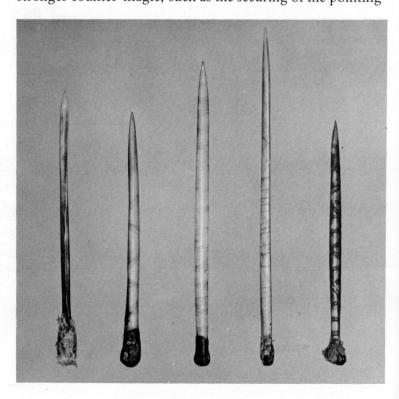

Pointing bones used in Central Australia

bone or the carrying out of ritual performances, was adopted.

The power of magic was further demonstrated through the talents of medicine-men. Medicine-men were usually not sorcerers—their efforts were directed at curing sicknesses, finding out the causes of death, making rain (or stopping it), and predicting the future. Sickness was believed to be the result of an evil spirit entering the body and had to be cured by removing the evil spirit. Here the services of the medicine-man were required. By rubbing or sucking the affected part a cure was attempted. Usually the medicine-man managed to produce a bone or piece of stick supposed to have come from the sick person and which was claimed to be responsible for the malady. In fact the medicine-men often were able to bring about a cure because of the psychological effect of their work, and they became greatly respected.

Minor illnesses were often treated by first-aid measures. Various plants were crushed and soaked in water to provide a fluid to relieve the effects of stomach troubles, snake-bites,

Kurdaitja shoes, worn to cover up tracks

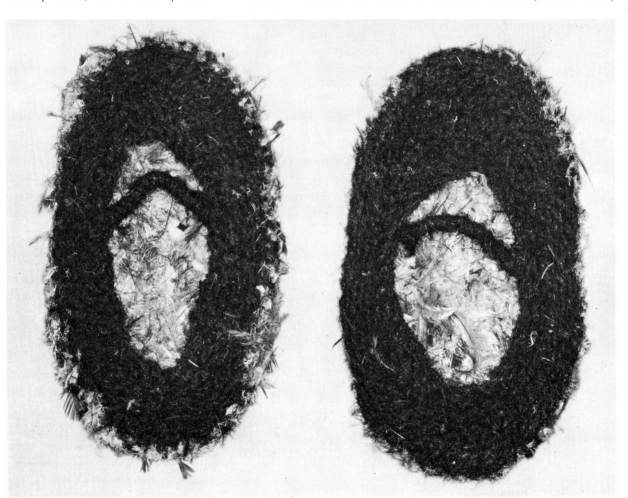

and injuries. Blood was drawn from the patient to help
relieve head-aches, and tourniquets were applied to lessen
pain. Aches and pains were also treated by the application of
heat, with the sick person either lying in hot sand or receiv-
ing steam treatment. Some illnesses were more difficult to
cure—eye-troubles, common among a people exposed to
dust and glare, were like this, and fractured limbs, although
often splinted, seldom mended well.

The Corroboree and its Artists

It would be a mistake to suppose that an Aborigine's life was
made continually grim by the prospect of sickness or the fear
of magical power being worked against him. Nor did the

Aborigines at play kicking a ball (Mid-19th
century, S. T. Gill)

PALTI DANCE

The Palti Dance by G. F. Angas. The performers painted themselves like skeletons and went through a range of gestures, shaking their legs and accompanying the movements with a loud noise. The end of each act was proclaimed by a tremendous shout

A dance known as the Kuri Dance, being performed in South Australia in the 1840s

ritual duties expected of him make him over-serious and reserved. He found many simple pleasures in daily life and these contributed to his good humour and temperament. Pleasure could be found and expressed in the music and dancing of the corroboree, which was usually a non-sacred occasion lacking the restrictions which applied to the performing and witnessing of ritual ceremonies. The corroboree centred on the day-to-day experiences of the people, dramatizing the affairs of humans and natural things through singing, dancing, and noise-making.

The music in the corroboree, and in the rituals, was made by simple means. In some tribes the Aborigines merely slapped their thighs to make the sound. In others pieces of wood, sometimes boomerangs, were struck together to provide the rhythmic beat for dancing. Bundles of gum leaves fastened around the ankles and arms enabled the Aborigine to imitate the rustling of an emu's feathers. The most distinctive sounds were the wailing chants of the Aborigines themselves or the droning notes of the *didjeridu,* the long pipe made from a bamboo or a eucalyptus branch. This instrument was restricted to certain northern parts of Australia. A skilled blower of the *didjeridu* was not always easy to find, and a person who could blow it well, never seeming to stop for breath and capable of producing notes of two different pitches, was in great demand.

The songman, too, was highly regarded. He was a special performer who composed songs to describe day-to-day events and whose extensive repertoire was enriched by songs handed down to him by his ancestors. Like the skilled *didjeridu* player, he was often asked to perform for other groups, and was paid for his services. There were specialist leaders in dancing as well. This was a central part of the corroboree and often involved a great deal of miming, especially of the actions of animals.

Language and Communication

Thus the Aborigines used various art forms to express themselves in corroborees and sacred ceremonies. These art forms were the usual means of communicating feelings and ideas on such occasions. At most other times, of course, communication was carried out by normal speech. There were a great number of different languages spoken, possibly about six hundred in all; but they had a general similarity, except perhaps for the Tasmanian ones. These languages were unlike those spoken in other countries, and because of this and of their apparent long usage it seems that they developed in Australia itself. They were often rich in meaning and vocabulary, especially in relation to the natural world around them. To understand any of them, it is necessary to be aware of the way the Aborigines lived and thought. Words were

Applying body decorations for the Pukamuni ceremony, Melville Island

often built up to a considerable length, and were spoken in voices of a reasonably high pitch.

Since there were so many spoken languages but no written language, it was often difficult for an Aborigine to communicate beyond his own tribe. Message-sticks carried between the tribes in fact had no messages written on them, but were to help identify the bearer and give him some authority. A common method of getting over the language difficulty was to employ sign language, which was extensive and effective. Signs were made with the hands or by facial

Two message-sticks used in Western Australia

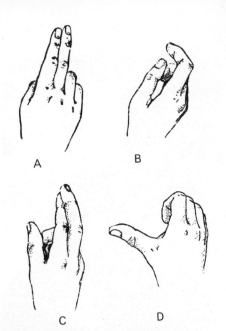

Hand signs used in Central Australia:
Figures A and B show signs for a small
kangaroo, C the sign for a kangaroo rat,
D for an opossum

(Below) An artist making a brush for
painting, Snake Bay, Melville Island

or body movements. These could also be used within a tribe
to convey secret meanings between members of a group and
to give messages when hunting. By this means considerable
'conversations' could be carried on. Another form of communication was by smoke-signals—these, like message-
sticks, conveyed no actual message, but were pre-arranged
signs useful in hunting and in fixing the location of a camp.
They were also made by a visitor to announce his presence
in a strange territory.

Visual Art

Finally, there were other important ways in which the
Aborigines expressed themselves—ways which can be called
visual art. This term refers mainly to the techniques of painting, shaping, and carving, carried out on wood, rock surfaces, or the ground; such things as making designs on skin
cloaks and modelling with beeswax were less common.

Aboriginal art reflected the everyday experiences of the
people, but its greatest inspiration came from the sacred life,
rich in its stories of the Dreamtime, totemic beliefs, and the
spirit-world. In art deriving from these things, the Aborigines were doing more than just making representations. They
were expressing their beliefs in a visual way and linking
themselves to the spirit world. Their art was 'sung' as much
as painted or engraved, and by singing or chanting as they

An example of old art—an engraved spiral from the James Range, Central Australia

worked they gave their art a religious meaning. This brought them closer to the spirit-heroes and the things in nature they wished to influence. Aboriginal art was most often art with a strong purpose, art which tried to communicate ideas and not act as some kind of photograph. So an Aborigine reverently re-painting sacred designs in a rockface was renewing their power and his own contact with the Dreamtime. An Aborigine who painted a representation of an emu hunt was trying to influence the result of such a hunt.

It is difficult to understand a good deal of Aboriginal visual art unless one is aware that it is symbolic in form. Usually it does not attempt to show exact likenesses of things, and many of its patterns and designs have thus been meaningless to people from another cultural background. Aboriginal art has reserved its hidden meaning for those who have the ritual

Spirit figures painted on Nourlangie rock face, Northern Territory

knowledge and experience to understand it. To an Aborigine, art lived. Re-tracing a painting in ochre could bring an increase in the animal and plant species in the painting, but leaving the painting unattended for a long time and allowing it to fade could lead to the failure of rains, a decline in food, and the possibility of death.

There was quite some variation in the type and amount of visual art practised throughout the continent. The Tasmanian Aborigines seem to have done very little, for only a few rock

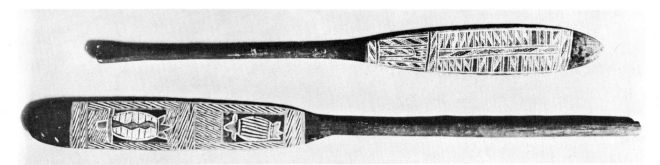

Arnhem Land paddles decorated with a
turtle design

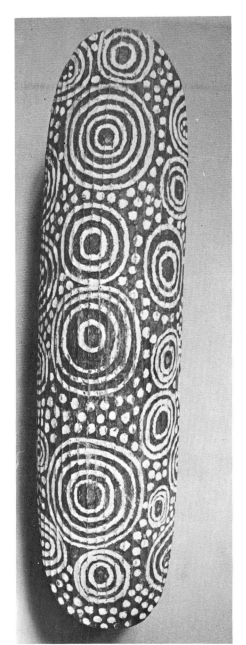

(Left) A decorated shield from Central
Australia

engravings and some bark paintings have survived. In the
drier areas of the mainland art was neither extensive nor
diverse, probably because the Aborigines there spent a more
wandering life in search of food. Nevertheless they made
rock engravings and paintings (often of geometrical design),
designs on weapons, and also fine ground and body painting
for ritual purposes. In Eastern Australia there was art on rock
surfaces, sometimes quite extensive. This region was also
noted for its carved trees and ground patterns for initiation
purposes. But it was in the northern parts of the continent
that Aboriginal art really flourished. In the Kimberleys were
the great rock paintings of the ancestral Wandjina figures, the
creator-heroes who were responsible for rain-making. In
Arnhem Land visual art was especially fine. Here the Aborigines spent time in decorating ceremonial objects and in
painting and engraving on rock and bark surfaces, leaving
some magnificent examples of their work. Notable were the
ancient figure paintings of the Mimis, small spirit people
who were pictured in active scenes. There were examples of
'X-ray art', in which animals were painted showing internal
organs as well as their external form, and highly decorative
bark paintings, frequently done on the inside of bark hut
shelters and inspired by the numerous religious cults of the
area.

In this chapter a broad survey has been made of the non-
material world of the Aboriginal people. Many words can
be used to summarize it, not least the words stable, well-
organized, religious, and artistic. What others can be used?
And how well have non-Aborigines understood that world?
How well did the Aborigines adjust to the Australian environment? How much of a disadvantage, or advantage, was
it that they were so isolated from other societies? Were they
at all a 'stone age' people? Were they a happy people? All
these questions, and others, come to mind when thinking
about Aboriginal society.

An Aboriginal petroglyph (rock carving)

The Lightning Brothers, painted on a cave wall, Delamere Station, Northern Territory. Yagtchadbulla, on the left, is about 3.5 metres high; with his brother Tcaibuinji he was associated with rain

An example of X-ray art—a kangaroo painted on a rock-face in Central Arnhem Land

These questions should be thought about carefully, and there may be a number of answers to them. Yet one thing has now become clear: much of Aboriginal society as it existed when Europeans began to settle in Australia no longer survives, and will not re-appear. The reasons for this can be found in what happened after Europeans began to settle in 1788, when the story of the human occupation of Australia, like the continent itself, was already very old.

1 See the section on the Local Group, the Family, and Kinship.
2 A. A. Abbie: op. cit., p. 208.
3 F. D. McCarthy: op. cit., p. 115
4 H. Basedow: op. cit., p. 272.

4

Aborigines and Whites: the Breaking Down of Aboriginal Society

Instructions issued in September, 1622 for two Dutch ships heading for the Australian coast

You will moreover go ashore in various places and diligently examine the coast in order to ascertain whether or no it is inhabited, the nature of the land and the people, their towns and inhabited villages, the divisions of their kingdoms, their religion and policy, their wars, their rivers, the shape of their vessels, their fisheries, commodities and manufactures, but specially to inform yourselves what minerals, such as gold, silver, tin, iron, lead, and copper, what precious stones, pearls, vegetables, animals and fruits, these lands yield and produce.

J. E. Heeres:
The Part Borne by the Dutch in the Discovery of Australia 1606–1765, London, 1899, p. 19

Two hundred years ago the Aborigines were the sole occupiers of the Australian continent. They had been resident there for many centuries, and they saw very little reason for change. A hundred years after white settlement began their ownership of huge areas of the continent was at an end. A people who had been masters of the land for so long found themselves struggling for survival as a race. Almost everywhere white settlement had proved overpowering. What had happened?

White people have usually explained their quickly established supremacy in Australia by claiming a higher material culture and greater natural abilities than the Aborigines. Occasionally they may refer to the comparatively small Aboriginal population, the effects of white man's diseases, and perhaps the effectiveness of European firearms. But generally the reasons are not greatly thought about. The story of what has happened between Aborigines and other people has been put in the background of Australian history.

The Explorers

The story, of course, does not just begin with Europeans in Australia. There were the seamen, already mentioned, who

An artist's impression of the arrival of European ships in Australian waters—the ships of Torres north of Australia at the beginning of the 17th century

An incident on Cape York Peninsula in 1756, involving a Dutch exploring party

In the morning of the 27th our men went ashore again for the purpose of attempting to get hold of one or two natives, but did not succeed in doing so that day, because they landed too late to lure the natives to the beach. Early in the morning of the 28th they again landed in order to execute their plan; on their arrival the natives came up to them dancing and singing, sat down close to them, laid aside their so-called assagays or weapons, and again enjoyed the liquor with which our men plied them. While they were thus making merry, our men seized hold of two of them, upon which the others jumped to their feet, snatched up their assagays and began to throw them at our people without, however, wounding any one; except that the ship's clerk, who in flying tried to seize one of the natives round the body, was in the scuffle slightly wounded in the hand; upon this our men fired a volley, wounding one of the natives, who thereupon all of them fled into the bush.

J. E. Heeres: *op. cit.*, p. 94.

(Left) Part of Dampier's description of the Aborigines on the north-west coast of Australia. (After the account in his *New Voyage Round the World*, 1697)

came to the northern shores and established limited but fairly orderly contact with the Aborigines. There were also the Dutch, who reached parts of the Australian coast early in the seventeenth century. Having become established in the Indonesian islands and being anxious to find trade further afield, the Dutch were probably the first white people the Aborigines had seen. Contacts between the two peoples were very limited, for the Dutchmen made only fleeting visits to the coasts. For their part they had been instructed to be careful in any contact they might make with the people—they must not spoil any chance of trade that might occur in the strange south land. They returned from their explorations, however, to report that there was no chance of trade, for the land seemed miserable and full of flies. The Aborigines were unimpressed by the trinkets shown to them and expressed resentment towards the new arrivals, who attempted to kidnap some of them. Fear and hostility were present on both sides, and relations between the groups were occasionally marked by bloodshed.

The Aborigines found that Europeans continued their interest in Australia. In 1688 and 1699 the buccaneering Englishman William Dampier visited the north-west coast, and added to the impressions already given by the Dutch. He gave Europeans a more detailed version of the life of the Aborigines. In the absence of more accurate and reasoned accounts, Dampier's views became widely known and accepted. His lack of understanding led him to a disgust of Aboriginal life, and he influenced many more to the same conclusion. His well-known description helped to established the misguided and unchanging beliefs and attitudes—the stereotypes—about Aborigines that white people were to hold in the future.

The inhabitants of this country are the miserablest people in the world. The Hodmadods of Monomatapa, though a nasty people, yet for wealth are gentlemen to these; who have no houses and skin garments, sheep, poultry, and fruits of the earth, ostrich eggs, etc., as the Hodmadods have; and setting aside their human shape, they differ but little from brutes. They are tall, straight-bodied and thin, with small, long limbs. They have great heads, round foreheads, and great brows. Their eye-lids are always half closed, to keep the flies out of their eyes, they being so troublesome here that no fanning will keep them from coming to one's face;...So that, from their infancy, being thus annoyed with these insects, they do never open their eyes as other people do; and therefore they cannot see far, unless they hold up their heads as if they were looking at somewhat over them.

They have great bottle-noses, pretty full lips and wide mouths, the two fore-teeth of their upper jaw are wanting in all of them, men and women, old and young: neither have they any beards. They are long-visaged, and of a very unpleasing aspect, having no one graceful feature in their faces. Their hair is black, short, and curled, like that of the negroes; and not long and lank.... The colour of their skins, both of their faces and the rest of their body, is coal black, like that of the negroes of Guinea.

They have no sort of clothes, but the piece of the rind of a tree ty'd lyke a girdle about their waists, and a handful of long grass, or three or four small green boughs, full of leaves, thrust under their girdle to cover their nakedness.

They have no houses, but lye in the open air without any covering the earth being their bed and the heaven their canopy. Whether they cohabit one to one woman, or promiscuously, I know not. But they do live in companies, twenty or thirty men, women and children together. Their only food is a small sort of fish, which they get by making wares of stone across little coves or branches of the sea; every tide bringing in the little fish, and there leaving them a prey to these people, who constantly attend there to search at low water.

...I did not perceive that they did worship anything. These poor creatures have a sort of weapon to defend their ware or fight with their enemies, if they have any that will interfere with their poor fishery. They did endeavour with their weapons to frighten us who, lying ashore, deterr'd them from one of their fishing places. Some of them had wooden swords, others had a sort of lances. The sword is a piece of wood shaped somewhat like a cutlass. The lance is a long strait pole, sharp at one end, and hardened afterwards by heat. I saw no iron, nor any other sort of metal; therefore it is probable they use stone hatchets....

How they get their fire I know not but probably, as Indians do, out of wood.

It was some time before Aborigines had much further contact with white explorers. The most important of these explorers proved to be another Englishman, Lieutenant James Cook, who in 1770 examined the east coast of Australia and its people. He wrote more favourably of the Aborigines: '...they may appear to some to be the most wretched people upon Earth, but in reality they are far...happier than we Europeans'. Although their material culture seemed poor and inadequate to him, Cook admired their peaceful approach and disposition.

White Settlement

Eighteen years later Captain Arthur Phillip arrived with white convict settlers on the coast that Cook had explored. No one could foresee at that time how much of an impact white settlement was going to have on the life of the people who already lived there. The Aborigines showed some surprise at the arrival of the new settlers, especially the Aboriginal women and children, who preferred to hide on seeing them. There was little attempt to oppose settlement; the Aborigines were peaceful and somewhat attracted to Governor Phillip, who behaved in a kindly fashion towards them. He tried to carry out the official instructions given to him by the British government, which hoped to see harmonious relations existing between the races and to extend the protection of British law to the Aborigines. Phillip had an unusual advantage in trying to bring this about, for the Aborigines admired him even more as a leader because his missing front tooth was a sign of status to them.

Troubles, however, soon began. The whites showed that their settlement was going to be a permanent one, and the Aborigines became resentful. Neither group could understand each other's customs. Aboriginal ways were thought to be primitive and uncivilized, and there was no understanding of the organized social system of the Aboriginal people nor of the great importance of religion in their lives. Soon physical clashes occurred between the two races, and fearful whites began to want the Aborigines to keep away from their settlement.

Phillip's early anxiety to befriend the Aborigines, and his willingness to do so even after he himself had been wounded by a spear, soon gave way to exasperation, which after the spearing of his personal huntsman, led him to demand blood and organize an expedition of revenge. Phillip seemed puzzled by the Aborigines, and disappointed that the whites could not 'civilize' them. The hope of Phillip had been that the whites would teach the Aborigines the ways of the Europeans. The Aborigines, however, remained unattracted to a majority of the white man's ways, although one of them, Benelong, accompanied Governor Phillip on his return to England and easily adopted the clothes, manners, and speech of the white man. The whites became disillusioned. Although Governor Lachlan Macquarie later tried to help the process of civilizing the Aborigines by establishing a school for them at Parramatta and a small farm at Port Jackson, there were many whites by this time who believed that little could be done to civilize the Aborigines. They thought it did not matter much if the Aborigines began to die out as a race, and that tough methods had to be employed to prevent continued clashes between the two groups.

Racial Clash and the Question of Land

Why were the Aborigines not really attracted to European ways and why did clashes occur? The Aborigines undoubtedly could see little use in much that the white man did. They had no need to cultivate the soil, since they could procure enough food from the existing native plants and could live quite well without domesticated animals. As for the white man's religion and learning, they had no need for them either—they had their own explanations of the world around them, and found the European answers puzzling. In fact, it was the Aborigines themselves who proved good teachers. They showed white settlers the trees which supplied the best timbers for various purposes and how to cut and treat bark for use in hut-making. They also showed them how to obtain bark fibre, which was greatly valued for making rope, and other ways of the bush. Above all they proved excellent guides in strange country, being invaluable companions to whites on journeys of exploration.

The whites claimed that clashes occurred because the Aborigines were naturally wicked and loved fighting. The claim was not accurate. The Aborigines in their own society were a peaceful people who fought little. Fighting among them was usually on a very limited scale, and often stopped when the first blood was drawn. Inter-tribal fighting scarcely occurred, and they seem to have had nothing like the kind of wars known among European people, in which territory was sought. For their part, the Aborigines could scarcely have been impressed by happenings among the whites—convict society offered daily examples of harshness and unpleasantness, of ill-treatment by whites of their fellow men.

White people also claimed that the Aborigines had no idea of land ownership, therefore white settlers could not be dispossessing them. Why, it was asked, did the Aborigines resent the new arrivals so much?

Part of the answer was already apparent to one of the early governors, Governor King. He realized that loss of land was a major reason for trouble, although settlers continued for many years to make the claim that the Aborigines had no land of their own. They would not learn from the example of Benelong, the Aborigine they knew best, who repeatedly declared that the island of Me-mul (Goat Island), near Sydney Cove, was his own and his family's home, to which he was deeply attached.[1]

The Aborigines' ties to the land were really very strong. To be forced from their tribal and local group lands meant that they lost their spiritual homes as well as the areas from which their food supply came. The feelings of the Aborigines must have been intense as white settlers and stock began to occupy such land, driving off the game, destroying the vegetation, fouling waterholes, and caring nothing for the sacred places. The real nature of what the whites were doing has been clearly shown by a modern writer:

> For Aborigines…land is a spiritual thing, a phenomenon from which culture and religion derive. It is not sellable or buyable. Land is not private property…Land was and is endowed with a magical quality, involving a relationship to the sun and the water and the earth and the animals all

An illustration published in 1836 of Piper, who accompanied Major Mitchell on an exploring expedition

PIPER.

(Opposite) Two scenes of Aborigines at Botany Bay, published in the *Voyage of Governor Phillip to Botany Bay* (1789). In these exaggerated scenes the Aborigines are pictured as 'noble savages', at a time when whites regarded them with approval. Compare these pictures with those on page 82, in which obviously different feelings are held by the artist

put together—for the collective use of all. The notion of a fence to separate portions of the land was unknown to them, for fences defaced the land. They could not, and some still cannot, understand the concept of making land into private property and giving its 'owners' the right to bar everyone else.... And so bloody conflict and massacre developed . . . because whites 'took' what Aborigines did not comprehend could be 'taken'.[2]

As white settlement increased after 1800, clashes between whites and Aborigines continued over possession of the land. To the British government and the governors in New South Wales who represented it, the whole matter was simple. The land was held to belong to the British Crown. The people who inhabited it, of both races, were claimed to be British subjects. The Aborigines were not consulted; for them there was no choice. They were declared to be under the protection of the law, but this proved little. In fact it was the white man who clamoured for protection and who received it most.

Matters became worse when settlers, encouraged by the prospects of the wool trade with Britain and by the crossing of the Blue Mountains, began to occupy land further out from the coast. Once again the Aborigines were simply denied any right to the land. Sometimes they reacted violently, spearing sheep or even the settlers themselves. Inevitably, clashes ended in the dispossession of Aboriginal land and the subjection of the people.

By the 1830s relations between Aborigines and Europeans had reached a critical stage. In New South Wales there were great stretches of country taken from the Aborigines. On the edge of settlement serious conflict occurred from time to time, reaching its peak in northern New South Wales, where in 1838 a group of station-hands killed twenty-eight bound Aborigines in an incident which has become known as the Myall Creek Massacre. In this case, unlike many others, a conviction was obtained against seven white station-hands who were responsible. The station-hands were hanged for their crime, despite sympathy for them from the white community. It was clear that many whites now shared the feelings of a writer who a few years previously had declared: 'Speaking of them collectively, it must be confessed I entertain very little more respect for the aborigines of New Holland, than for the ourang-outang . . . .' They would have agreed with his further opinion: '. . . We have taken possession of their country, and are determined to keep it . . . .'[3]

The Other Colonies

Further south, in Van Diemen's Land, the position was even worse. In 1804, soon after white settlement began, some 'innocent and well disposed' Aborigines were murdered at Risdon Cove, which started a chain reaction of unpleasant incidents between the two races. Lawless sealers and con-

A wordless proclamation issued by Governor Arthur about 1830 to discourage fighting between black and white

(Below) Truganini, sometimes claimed to be the last of the Tasmanian Aborigines

(Opposite) Aborigines in New South Wales drinking *bool* or sugar water, and Aborigines fighting in Sydney. These scenes by C. Rodius, c. 1836, reveal as much about how white settlers regarded Aborigines as they reveal about the actual condition of the Aboriginal people near white settlements. Compare the earlier, pleasant scenes on page 80.

victs, in murdering the Aborigines and kidnapping their womenfolk, filled the hearts of the Aboriginal people with hatred and desire for revenge. The settlers wanted to solve the Aboriginal question once and for all; some of them simply wanted the extermination of all Aborigines on the island. They began to look to the governor, Lieut.-Colonel Arthur, to take strong action. After some futile early measures, Arthur sought to outlaw the Aborigines from the settled districts. He soon declared martial law. In 1830 he tried an amazing military operation, in which five thousand whites tried to drive any remaining Aborigines into the Tasman Peninsula. This 'Black War', as it was called, said to cost a great sum of money, was a hopeless failure—only two Aborigines were captured. It was left to George Robinson, a brick-layer of simple faith whose peaceful manner led to friendly relations with the Aborigines, to take the last of the Tasmanian Aborigines to Flinders Island. Here there was

A clash between members of Grey's exploring expedition and Aborigines near Hanover Bay, north-western Australia, in 1837

some safety for them, but, removed from their tribal lands and urged to accept strange European customs and learning, they continued to die out. By 1850 hardly any of them survived.

In Western Australia, where settlement began in the 1820s, the early aims of protecting the Aborigines and giving them the benefits of white men's learning and religion were, as elsewhere, soon outweighed by other concerns. Governor Stirling allowed whites to take strong measures against any Aborigines who were said to cause trouble, and personally took part in the 'Battle of Pinjarra' to punish Aborigines of the Murray River tribe south of Perth. Once again the Aborigines were unable to withstand the pressure of white settlers, who were determined to occupy the land and were able to win out by force of arms if need be.

It was at Port Phillip Bay in 1835 that an effort was made to see that justice was done to the Aborigines over the ownership of the land. John Batman, an ambitious pastoralist from Van Diemen's Land, was anxious to gain good grazing land near the River Yarra for himself and his partners. Unable to get official permission to settle there, Batman solved matters by bargaining with the Aborigines for a large area of land. Batman's treaty was declared illegal by the New

An Aboriginal rock painting depicting the coming of the white man

South Wales governor, and although white settlement at Port Phillip expanded quickly and profitably, neither Batman nor the Aborigines obtained any benefit from the deal. Aborigines soon suffered: tribal life decayed and they died in hundreds.

Great hopes were held that the colony of South Australia, founded in 1836, should be free of the racial troubles that had occurred in colonies already settled. There were officials, such as Lord Glenelg, in the British government of the time who were anxious to give the Aborigines much greater protection and the blessings of British ways and the Christian religion. Although a Protector of Aborigines was appointed for the new colony, and a good deal of talk about kindly treatment of the Aborigines took place, efforts to help, and results, were feeble. The Kaurna tribe in the neighbourhood of Adelaide was soon shattered as a unit. Tribes which survived longer felt no real benefit from the occasional educational, missionary, and welfare attempts made by the whites. Far from being a model colony in its treatment of the Aboriginal people who lived there, South Australia resembled the other colonies in the rapid occupation of Aboriginal lands, the physical violence which occurred between the

(Above) A group of Aborigines about 1850, influenced by white settlement

A scene in the conflict between white and black—an attack on a store dray (S. T. Gill)

races, and the settlers' ignorance about the nature of Aboriginal society.

In the northern parts of Australia the Aborigines and whites engaged in an often violent struggle. In the Moreton Bay district (part of the future colony of Queensland) there were a number of incidents in which poisoned flour and guns were used by white settlers. As settlement advanced, the Native Police force came into prominence—it frequently used brutal methods to enforce peace as pastoral holdings were developed. Only on stations where Aborigines were used as a labour force did their presence seem at all welcome; elsewhere they were likely to be attacked indiscriminately. In the Northern Territory things were no better. From the time of John McDouall Stuart's explorations, the Northern Territory was a scene of racial conflict, a conflict marked by mistrust and violence in which guns, spears, and staghounds often featured. Only feeble efforts were made by administrators to calm the situation. Matters were left in the hands of the settlers themselves or entrusted to police at the head of punitive expeditions and forces of Native Police. The spearing of cattle would often be the reason for such an expedition, frequently leading to loss of life among the Aborigines.

The Impact of Settlement

The decline of the Aboriginal tribes was hastened by such measures, though it went on even where relations between the races were not violent but marked by friendship and trust on both sides. The decline occurred despite the setting up of ration-stations for the distribution of flour and blankets to Aborigines, and despite the work of missionary establishments and official Protectors of Aborigines.

At the heart of the decline was the land question already referred to. The declared attitude of the British government and the governments of each of the colonies remained clear— all the land belonged to the whites, even if they were not occupying it. They claimed that the land was waste and uncultivated, and that the settlers had the right to labour on it and own it. Even where some reserves were set aside for the Aborigines, the actual ownership of the reserves was claimed by the whites, and white pastoralists were often allowed to graze their stock there.

The Aboriginal people regarded white settlement as an unjustified intrusion on their lands. The white men's stock began to eat out the native grasses and to drive off kangaroos and emus, which provided essential meat food. The situation was made worse by the white pastoralists' determination to control the existing water-holes, water-holes which were soon fouled by stock. For the Aborigines the delicate balance between the population and the natural food supply was now upset. The white intruders showed no desire to compensate, and did not acknowledge the food-sharing practices found among the Aboriginal people themselves. The situation, of course, was more than just an economic one, for the Aborigines saw the whites and their stock occupying the sacred places, such as the totemic sites to which the Aborigines were deeply and reverently attached.

It was little wonder that Aborigines sometimes struck back in anger, spearing stock which were on their hunting-grounds and which they thus believed they were entitled to hunt. A bitter racial conflict began, in which the Aborigine was at a disadvantage in arms. The first interest of white governments came to be to provide protection *from* the Aborigines, rather than *of* them. This could be done by punitive expeditions or by legal proceedings.

One Law for All

In legal proceedings the Aborigine was at a further disadvantage. Due to problems about the oath, Aboriginal evidence was at first not admitted in the white man's law courts; when later it was, legal processes still weighed heavily against justice for Aborigines. No Aborigine ever appeared as prosecutor, juror, or judge. He was completely subject to the court procedure and legal code of the European, both of which were entirely foreign to his experience and understanding. The Aborigine was a person in a strange situation, with his language often not understood and his own tribal law not taken into account. His confusion was shown by his tendency to look for, and give, the answer required by the prosecution. He was also a victim of the bias and prejudice of the courts, which were anxious to uphold the position of the white settlers and which admitted no Aboriginal ownership of the land. Beyond this was the system of punishment adopted by the courts, a system which he could not understand and which left him bewildered and fearful.

The failure of white settlers to take Aboriginal law and customs into account had serious consequences. The Aboriginal people were bound by strict obligations which were not recognized by the whites. Disputes were settled by different means, involving actual or ceremonial punishments. The intention was to restore the life of the group to its peaceful, settled state as soon as possible. The whites were unable or unwilling to understand the Aboriginal system. The resulting ignorance of the obligations which began to apply to white people as soon as they trespassed on Aboriginal lands or had relations with Aboriginal women often led to violent reactions against them.

The Break-up of Aboriginal Society

Aboriginal life could not stay as it was in the face of determined white colonists. It could not adapt itself to the loss of land which had a spiritual as well as economic value. Beliefs and social customs were inevitably weakened, and the morale of the people weakened, too. No longer did their social system support them; no longer did they carry out their duties as in the old days. The spiritual basis of Aboriginal life was lost.

The whites' desire to educate and convert the Aborigines only hastened this break-up of Aboriginal society. Whites saw the Aborigines as a people who had declined in culture to a primitive state. They ridiculed Aboriginal beliefs and customs and tried to replace them with their own. But white people's beliefs and customs were those of a very different culture, puzzling to the Aborigines and not satisfying to them. There seemed little meaning in the new ways, and those Aborigines who had much contact with them were torn between respect for a white missionary or employer and respect for the secret life of their own people, both making claims for their loyalty. Younger Aborigines were understandably confused. Their position was usually not appreciated by whites who, instead, criticized their apparent unwillingness and inability to live according to 'civilized' ways and their desire to follow the traditional ways which

Wybalenna, the settlement at Flinders Island, 1847. This was one of the early institutions set up for Aborigines

Two groups of white squatters, as sketched by a young Aborigine in the 19th century

(Below) Aborigines of the Grafton district, New South Wales, in 1895

seemed so backward. There followed a serious disruption of Aboriginal social life. The kinship obligations which carefully regulated Aboriginal society were either ignored or not understood at all by whites, and Aborigines found it increasingly difficult to observe these obligations. White missionaries, by preventing initiation ceremonies where they could, prevented young men being accepted by the older men as full tribal members and adults. Marriages which cut across the traditional kinship rules were encouraged by whites, and other patterns of behaviour, so important in keeping Aboriginal social life regulated and of high order, were broken down.

White settlers were often preoccupied with the material problems of colonial life. The Aborigines seemed part of a strange land which was not easy to live in. Fear of the Aborigines became a common factor in the colonists' attitude towards them, especially in thinly settled parts of the country. Another problem was that convicts and former convicts were among the first to make contact with the Aborigines in older districts—their feelings were harsh and their habits, such as drunkenness, were poor models for the Aborigines to copy. The Aborigines found adjustment difficult—their world was one in which tradition was highly important, with no emphasis on change as in white society. The sight of the first white settlers must have been a remarkable one—the

Aborigines in New South Wales at the end of the 19th century.

An Aranda man's sorrow about what happened to a sacred site

The Ilbalintja soak has been defiled by the hands of white men. Two white men came here to sink a well. They put down into the sacred soak plugs of gelignite, to blast an opening through the hard rock at the bottom. But the rock was too hard for them. They had to leave without having been able to shatter it; they took ill soon afterwards and died.

And now the soak has almost gone dry. No longer do men pluck up the grass and the weeds and sweep the ground clean around it; no longer do they care for the resting place of Karora. Bushes have grown up on the very edge of the soak, and there is no one to uproot them. The bandicoots have vanished from the tall grass in the mulga thicket. Our young men do no longer care for the traditions of their fathers; and their women bear no children. Soon the men of Ilbalintja will be no more; we shall all sleep in our graves as our forefathers do now.

There is little here for strangers to see; there is no mountain cave here, only a storehouse in a mulga tree. But though the soak has been forsaken by almost all our people, a few of us old men still care for it. It still holds me fast; and I shall tend it while I can: while I live, I shall love to gaze on this ancient soil.

T. G. H. Strehlow; *Aranda Traditions*, Melbourne, 1947, p. 31

Aborigines sometimes thought them to be the spirits of their forefathers returning to visit them.

After the stage of clashes with the white settlers, there came the break-up of tribal life. The earlier stage had been marked by occupation of the land and occasional raiding and killing of stock, often when food was scarce; the latter stage was one in which the Aborigines were forced to adjust to white settlement as best they could. With their former control of their environment now gone, they drifted to the edge of towns, settlements, and mission stations, attracted by white man's material objects and his food, drink, and tobacco. In this situation their health and spirit weakened.

Disease

The factor of disease in the break-up of tribal life proved to be very significant. Before the visits of the Macassan people and the coming of the whites, the Aborigines were relatively free from disease, their chief troubles coming from eye and skin complaints. The marsupials they hunted did not transmit their diseases to man. But with the arrival of other people and their stock, new diseases, to which Aborigines had no natural resistance, were introduced. Leprosy, tuberculosis, and smallpox had a terrible effect, and milder diseases such as influenza, measles, whooping-cough, and the common cold were often just as deadly among a people who had no previous contact with them. Accounts reveal that in some tribes most, or all, of the children died from such diseases. Smallpox introduced by whites in the Sydney area spread along the Murray River into South Australia, and had a shattering effect on Aboriginal numbers. There seemed to be no remedy available to the Aboriginal people. The 'smallpox song' which they sang was powerless to prevent the spread of the disease, while elsewhere the death of the medicine-men and the destruction of medicinal herbs by introduced stock reduced the Aborigines' chances of survival even further. In many places the effects of disease had sharply reduced Aboriginal numbers even before white people settled in those areas.

The decline in Aboriginal numbers in the southern part of the continent during the nineteenth century became obvious to all. One observer recorded in 1886:

> Experience shows that a populous town will kill out the tribes which live near enough to visit it daily in from two to ten years. . . . In more sparsely-settled country the process is somewhat different and more gradual, but it leads to the same end. In the bush many tribes have disappeared, and the rest are disappearing. Towns destroy by drunkenness and debauchery; in the country, from fifteen to five-and-twenty per cent fall by the rifle; the tribe then submits, and diseases of European origin complete the process of extermination.[4]

This description is a general one, not accurate in all districts, and does not mention the efforts made by a determined few to prevent such happenings. A fairly common pattern, however, is clear.

Soothing the Dying Pillow

The apparent dying-out of the Aboriginal race at this time helped to bring an end to those earlier ideas, held mostly by whites living in the towns, of assimilation of the Aborigines into the white community. The attitude became one of 'soothing the dying pillow', in which the whites should make the passing of the Aborigines as peaceful as possible. To the whites who cared, this seemed the worthiest thing to do. It was also a policy of despair. The editor of a Melbourne journal in 1868 summed up the attitude:

> Let us make their passage to the grave as comfortable as possible—let us do our best to civilize them and convert them to Christianity; but let us not flatter ourselves that, up to the present at any rate, we have succeeded. Something may be done with the half-castes, but the case of the full-blooded aboriginal is, we fear, hopeless.[5]

In practice the task of making the passage to the grave as comfortable as possible was left to the mission stations, controlled either by religious groups or by governments. Only a few whites, however, had much energy for this, and the failure of earlier policies towards Aborigines gave governments a good excuse to do very little. Their actions were mainly confined to gathering the surviving Aborigines in the southern districts on reserves and mission stations, where they could be supplied with medicine, shelter, a minimum of food, and the customary blankets. In these places Aborigines could be kept away from the white community. This policy of segregation, the governments declared, would enable them to avoid contact with the worst of the white settlers. To white settlers themselves, this must have seemed a good idea, for it removed from their neighbourhood people whom they did not really like and whose rights to the land they totally denied. The policy of 'soothing the dying pillow' was an easy one to accept, for it helped to satisfy the few whites who were concerned about the condition of the Aboriginal people and indicated to other whites that the Aboriginal race would one day cease to trouble them.

Further Ideas of Protection

By the beginning of the twentieth century Aborigines had lost the struggle to save their land in all except the remote parts of the continent. They had no opportunity of determining their future, nor was their culture respected. White anthropologists were still only at the first stages in their research into Aboriginal life, and Aboriginal languages were still largely ignored. Knowledge about Aborigines was gathered only slowly by the few white people who regarded them as anything more than oddities or nuisances. For many whites things were seen in simple terms—'Bullocks and blacks won't mix'.

There were hopes, however, that the new federal government established for the Australian colonies in 1901 would mean a better deal for Aborigines. Some people even suggested that the new government should take over from the separate states the responsibility for all Aboriginal affairs. But things did not change very much. It was decided, for example, that Aborigines should not be counted in any federal census. Thus the original owners of the land were officially not counted or regarded as Australians. The new government had brought no new view on matters affecting the Aboriginal people, and it was left largely to the six states to administer Aboriginal affairs. Their policies reflected their concern for restrictive laws and segregation of Aborigines. A Queensland Act in 1897 set the pattern for these types of action. It gave white Protectors of Aborigines strong powers to control the lives of Aboriginal and part-Aboriginal people. It provided for reserves upon which these people should live, and controlled their movements and employment by whites. The same pattern was followed in Western Australia and South Australia, so that Aborigines who were no longer living under tribal conditions were often living on reserves closely supervised by the state government. In effect they became inmates of institutions.

The basis of the government policies for the 'protection' of Aborigines was thus the deliberate restriction of their rights as people. There was no attempt now, nor had there been in the past, to consider what Aborigines themselves wanted. The whites had always assumed that to adopt the standards and practices of the white community was the best thing for Aborigines. If Aborigines did not do that, it was said that they were lacking in ability. There was always the feeling that it was the Aborigines, not the whites, who had failed.

Troubles in the North

On the edge of European settlement relations between settlers and Aborigines still produced the examples of conflict and inhumanity that had occurred at earlier periods. In remote areas of the Northern Territory and Western Australia there were settlers and bushmen who were accustomed to shoot Aborigines on sight or turn their dogs loose at sundown. Some of the worst incidents were revealed by Dr W. E. Roth, who was asked to make a report to the Western Australian government in 1905. He revealed 'a most brutal and outrageous state of affairs' in the northern part of the state, including police corruption in the matter of Aboriginal ration allowances, the chaining together (by the neck) of arrested Aborigines and Aboriginal witnesses and prisoners, forced child labour and heavy sentences for children and adults convicted of killing cattle, discrimination in court proceedings, and a shortage of food.[6]

There was no effort by the white man in the north to hide his fierce determination to seize and hold the land. This brought him into opposition to some white city-dwellers, not because they questioned his right to the land but because they questioned the means that he used. Arguments sometimes ran in the newspapers over the issue. The northerners'

Aboriginal stockmen branding cattle at Sturt Creek, Northern Territory, at the end of the 19th century

A camp along the east-west railway line earlier this century

feelings were clear, and can be seen in a poem written by one of their supporters:

The civic merchant, snugly housed and fed,
Who sleeps each night on soft and guarded bed,
Who never leaves the city's beaten tracks,
May well believe in kindness to the blacks.
But he can never know, nor hardly guess,
The dangers of the pathless wilderness;
The rage and frenzy in the squatter's brain
When the speared bullocks dot the spreading plain;
The lust for vengeance in the stockman's heart
Who sees his horse lie slain by savage dart;

An Aboriginal chain gang going to work at Wyndham, Western Australia, about the turn of this century. The guard is on the extreme right

A police party with prisoners wearing neck chains, Ellery Creek, MacDonnell Ranges, Northern Territory, about 1900

The nervous thrill the lonely traveller feels
When round his camp the prowling savage steals;
Nor that fierce hate with which the soul is filled
When man must slaughter or himself be killed.

Ah! who shall judge? Not you, my city friend,
Whose life is free from all that can offend;
Who pass your days in comfort, ease, and peace,
Guarded by metropolitan police.
Ah! who shall judge the bushman's hasty crime
Both justified by circumstance and clime.
Could you, my friend, 'neath such assaults be still,
And never feel that wild desire to kill?
Steps in your own defence would you not take
When law is absent then your own laws make.[7]

The Commonwealth government became more involved with Aboriginal affairs after 1911, when it took over administration of the Northern Territory from South Australia. Its policy of protection resembled that found in several of the states. Every aspect of Aboriginal life was carefully regulated. The Aborigines' freedom of movement was greatly restricted; for many, life was centred on institutions established under government control, where the opportunity to make personal decisions and live in simple dignity was slight. Special conditions governed their employment, while their personal property remained under the control of the Chief Protector. The Protector, and not the children's parents, was also the legal guardian of the children.

Yet despite expert help at the beginning, the Commonwealth was no more able than the states to improve the situation. In many parts of the Territory there remained trouble between the races, trouble which was usually left to the police to solve as they saw fit. In places such as Arnhem Land, it was possible for Aborigines to live a better life, in more tribal conditions; around the white settlements and stations they camped in poverty, really welcome only when

Distributing rations to Aborigines in
South Australia, 1913

their labour was essential in the pastoral industry. The Commonwealth seemed to forget that they existed, until their
condition became publicized late in the 1920s. At that time
drought robbed many Aborigines of natural food supplies,
and brought complaints about their plight from some concerned whites in the south. More spirited complaints fol-

Part of a letter written in April 1924 by
William Taylor, an Aborigine unhappy
about mission employment and the
chance of obtaining land

*...I have lived at...Mission Stations, for a few years, until
I could live there no longer owing to the high cost of living,
and the very poor wages...ranging from 5/- to 7/- per day for
married men with families....I can hardly make both ends
meet on...14/- per day, but by going out shearing or doing
other piece work or contract work I seem to manage. Rations
and blankets to the aged and needy are of inferior quality, one
blanket for two married adults, rations unrefined sugar, second
rate flour and last grade tea. These are only supplied to the
aged full-blooded Aboriginal, and those in dire circumstances,
otherwise nil, and about land or farms, there should be
numerous reserves all over the state, but after inquiries and
applications to the Chief Protector of Aborigines for a grant
of land to which we are entitled by Act of Parliament, I have
been informed that certain reserves that I have applied for, do
not exist as reserves which means that they have been sold.
I suppose there are many like myself who would be only too
glad to get a block of land on which to maintain themselves,
but the Government will not give us a chance....*

lowed about another matter. Following the death in 1928 of a white miner in Central Australia, a police expedition set out to find the culprits and took heavy toll of Aboriginal lives in the vicinity. The reaction from city people devoted to Aboriginal welfare was bitter, and was hardly helped by an official report which justified the police shooting.

Such troubles awoke again the old arguments between whites in towns and those on the edge of settlement about how the Aborigines should be treated. There were those who still thought and spoke of the Aborigines as others had earlier, as a kind of animal, describing him as 'wild' or 'tame'. There were those who still took refuge in the belief that the Aborigines were dying out, despite evidence to the contrary. Even as late as 1938 the well-known worker for Aborigines on the Nullarbor, Daisy Bates, published her book under the title of *The Passing of the Aborigines*.

Malnutrition

There were many Aborigines whose lives were cut short by malnutrition and disease at this time. A doctor with much knowledge of the Aboriginal situation has claimed that malnutrition was the greatest long-standing damage inflicted by the whites and the one least acknowledged with regret; he referred to the belief that Aborigines could survive and maintain health on much less food than whites could.[8] With malnutrition went the question of health. Government and station rations were often inadequate. Flour, sugar, and tea were the usual items issued, along the pattern laid down in the previous century, when governments saw feeding-stations as a means of preventing Aboriginal hunger which might lead to the spearing of stock. The absence of protein foods damaged the health of Aborigines and was a cause of high infant mortality. Damp clothing and poor housing caused further suffering. Disease, especially tuberculosis, continued to be widespread and often fatal.

Some Signs of Change

The questions of malnutrition and disease, however, were not those that most concerned white people engaged in pastoral occupations in remote areas. When they expressed interest in Aboriginal affairs it was usually in terms of the labour question. Yet by the 1930s Aboriginal affairs were no longer of importance just on the frontier of settlement or on the reserves. Greater interest began to develop in the cities in matters relating to the Aboriginal people. It was stimulated by the newspaper reports of incidents in the Northern Territory. Aborigines along the Arnhem Land and nearby coast clashed with Japanese adventurers who came to search for pearls and trepang. Peaceful relations between the groups were often broken by arguments about Aboriginal women, and violence followed. In one incident at Caledon Bay in

1933 five Japanese were killed, while in others Aboriginal and white lives were lost. Uneasiness arose about the effects which missionaries were having on Aboriginal culture in various parts of Australia, and whether Aboriginal law should be taken into account in white law courts when Aborigines were involved. In southern states outright protests came from several groups anxious to promote the welfare of the Aboriginal people—they opposed the expeditions of punishment, the ill-treatment of Aboriginal witnesses, and the bias of the white courts.

In the southern states themselves there was little cause for satisfaction. Aborigines there had long been reduced to living in generally miserable conditions on reserves, mission stations, or at the edges of towns. They were subject to a policy of segregation which sought to keep them separate from the white community and which provided for close supervision of their daily lives. Their opportunities for achieving the same standards as the white community in fields such as education, health, and employment were very limited, and prejudice towards them was strong.

In the 1930s it was noticeable that the number of part-Aborigines was increasing. The states, however, also made part-Aborigines subject to strict laws, often going to great pains to define who should be regarded as of Aboriginal origin and thus subject to restrictive laws. Governments, it seemed, had little enthusiasm for great improvements in the situation of the Aboriginal people. There was an emphasis on what Aborigines could *not* do, and no willingness to allow them to determine their future for themselves.

By 1937 there were some signs of change. Several white and Aboriginal groups pressed for a change in the negative ideas of protection and sought a more positive approach from governments. The views of anthropologists became of greater importance. They were able to give a better understanding of Aboriginal affairs, revealing that the Aboriginal people living in poverty on the outskirts of towns, or on stations or reserves, were more than just items in a government policy, more than objects who were to be looked down on and pitied. They were members of a race which had established a unique culture in Australia. Their society had been well ordered and stable, in which traditions of sharing and religious feeling were strong. It was this kind of society which had been so much destroyed by European settlement, and whose members had not been protected by policies of protection. The great majority of the tribes had vanished. In Tasmania and Victoria the destruction had been complete. Elsewhere those who survived this process lived as second-class citizens. They had been given neither the time not the opportunity to adjust meaningfully and with dignity to the coming of the European to their country. Instead they were often forced to live in institutions, where facilities were inadequate and where there was little of the psychological comfort found in traditional life.

There was an effort now to revise the older policies. At a conference held in Canberra in 1937 it was affirmed that 'the destiny of the natives of Aboriginal origin, but not of the full-blood, lies in their ultimate absorption by the people of the Commonwealth'. Full-blood Aborigines were to be supervised on pastoral stations and reserves, while those living in the large reserves such as Arnhem Land could preserve the tribal way of life.

Some Views of the Past

By the beginning of the Second World War in 1939, the idea of assimilation of the Aboriginal people into the white community was becoming more widespread. There was talk now of citizenship for Aborigines. Yet protection was still the policy in practice, and racial prejudice against the Aboriginal people remained strong. The restrictive laws continued to produce examples of injustice and caused frustration and resentment among Aborigines. Their frustration and resentmant had become obvious at the time of the celebration in

Survivors of the Narrinyeri tribe at a mission station in South Australia, photographed between 1910 and 1915

1938 of the 150th Anniversary of the beginning of white settlement in Australia. The Aborigines Progressive Association declared that January 26 should be a day of mourning. It wanted to protest 'on the anniversary of the white man's seizure of our country against the callous treatment of our people during the past 150 years'. The president appealed for new laws for the education and care of Aborigines, and asked for a new policy which would raise Aborigines to full citizenship.

There was support from some members of the white population for the Association's claims about callous treatment. The noted writer and poet, Mary Gilmore, in a statement whose accuracy was denied by other whites but which she maintained was correct, declared that as a child she had seen Aborigines massacred in hundreds. They had been lying dead around poisoned waterholes, and she had seen hunting parties gather. Dogs had been imported from Europe because they were more savage. She had seen little children dead in the grass, and scalps of Aborigines paid for as if they were dingoes.[9]

The Association put forward its own claims on behalf of the Aborigines:

> You are the new Australians, but we are the old Australians. You came here only recently, and you took our land from us by force. You have almost exterminated our people, but there are enough of us remaining to expose the humbug of your claim, as white Australians, to be a civilized, progressive, kindly and humane nation....We do not wish to be regarded with sentimental sympathy, or to be 'preserved,' like koala bears, as exhibits; but we do ask for your real sympathy, and understanding....
>
> We ask you to teach our people to live in the modern age as modern citizens. Our people are good and quick in assimilating knowledge. Why do you deliberately keep us backward? Is it merely to give yourselves the pleasure of feeling superior? Give our children the same chances as your own, and they will do as well as white children. We ask you to be proud of the Australian Aborigines and not to be misled any longer by the superstition that we are a naturally backward and low race. This is a scientific lie, which has helped to push our people down and down into the mire.
>
> At worst, we are no more dirty, lazy, stupid, criminal or immoral, than white people. Also, your slanders against our race are moral lies, told to throw all the blame for our troubles on to us. You, who originally conquered us by guns against our spears, now rely on superiority of numbers to support your false claims of moral and intellectual superiority.[10]

In these words the Aboriginal view of white settlement and current policies was put forward, forcibly and with much feeling, just before the problems of the Second World War emerged.

1 S. Kittle: *Concise History of the Colony and Natives of New South Wales,* Edinburgh, 1814, p. 180.
2 C. M. Tatz: *Four Kinds of Dominion,* Armidale, N.S.W., 1972, p. 16.
3 Lt. Breton: *Excursions in New South Wales, Western Australia, and Van Diemen's Land...,* London, 1833, pp. 196, 200.
4 E. M. Curr: *The Australian Race,* Melbourne, 1886, Vol. 1, p. 209.
5 *Illustrated Melbourne Post*, 13 August, 1868.
6 Quotations from Dr Roth's Report can be found in M. M. Bennett: *The Australian Aboriginal as a Human Being*, London, 1930, pp. 63–7.
7 *South Australian Register*, 24 November, 1902.
8 Charles Duguid: *No Dying Race*, Adelaide, 1963, p. 138.
9 *Sydney Morning Herald*, 4 March, 1938.
10 *The Argus*, 13 January, 1938.

The Modern Period

By the year 1939, when the Second World War began, it was not difficult to see what had been the effects of one and a half centuries of white settlement in Australia on the Aborigines and their culture. In the more fertile parts of the continent there were cities, towns, and farmland clearly marked out on land which had traditionally belonged to the Aboriginal people. The population of Aborigines and part-Aborigines was about seventy thousand, most of them living outside the boundaries of city, town, and farmland. What had happened can be largely explained by the term 'the destruction of Aboriginal society'.[1] The period since white settlement began had been one of destruction of the Aborigines' society and of a decline in their numbers and hold over their country. In fact, the words destruction and decline seem to fit so much of what had happened since white colonization had occurred.

The next decades were to see more destruction and decline, but there were to be new terms, such as advancement, integration, and land rights, used by whites and their governments and by Aborigines themselves. By the 1980s there was a new mood and a new way of thinking in Aboriginal affairs, in which Aborigines, especially younger ones, were confronting the white population with the truth of what had happened in the past, and with demands for change. The story of the Aboriginal occupation of Australia—of the kind of society they established and of the breaking-down of that society—has been the subject of the previous chapters. The story should be continued by referring in outline to some of the developments after 1945 which may help to explain the situation in which Aborigines find themselves at present.

Aborigines and Government Policies after 1945

The Second World War had a great impact on the Aborigines. It delayed or cancelled government plans of action, while it gave many more Aborigines greater contact with whites, especially at army depots and other places where jobs were available. Aborigines had come increasingly to towns and cities. There they found work, and increased the need for governments to devise better policies in relation to Aborigines living in or near the white community, indeed for all Aborigines. Emphasizing the need was the increase in numbers of Aborigines and part-Aborigines, and the fact that

(Opposite top) A cottage on a government Aboriginal Reserve, 1956
(Opposite bottom) The interior of the same cottage

these people continued to be attracted to the larger centres of white population after the war ended in 1945.

Yet many restrictive laws survived after the war. The Aboriginal people still remained subject to special laws not applying to white people, and gaining freedom from the application of these laws was difficult. Conditions on reserves remained depressed. Aborigines lived in circumstances far worse than those of whites. In the north-west of New South Wales, for example, where natural food and other provisions were sometimes unobtainable, a typical day's diet on one government Aboriginal reserve was:

> Breakfast: Tea and damper. Dinner: Bread and jam, sometimes soup. Supper: Meat and bread or damper, tea.
> On the river bank near the same station: Tea and damper for every meal; occasionally saveloys for supper.

The situation was described further:

> The children in both cases suffer from impetigo (skin disease), running noses, susceptibility to colds, and general malnutrition . . . .
> Diet in the towns and their neighbourhood is a little better, but infants are given adult food much too young. Faulty feeding and lack of proper attention cause many deaths.[2]

Governments now had the task of actually bringing about the stated aim of assimilation. To make Aborigines legally, socially, and economically equal to whites demanded not only the removal of restrictive laws but also much greater attention to Aboriginal welfare. It also demanded something more difficult to achieve—a change of attitude on the part of whites towards the place of Aborigines in Australian society.

Some effort was made to get the Commonwealth and state governments to co-operate more closely in Aboriginal affairs. A conference in 1948 set the pattern for this, and important policy matters were henceforth decided by meetings between the Commonwealth and state officials. In 1951 the Commonwealth and the states agreed on the general principle of assimilation of Aborigines and part-Aborigines—all were 'expected eventually to attain the same manner of living as other Australians, and to live as members of a single Australian community'. In addition, welfare services and payments were introduced or increased, and missions were given greater assistance or taken over by governments. In 1965 the assimilation policy was re-stated. It became one of integration, so that the emphasis came not on the suppression of Aboriginal culture and the disintegration of the race, but on the right of Aborigines to choose to retain their culture and their identity as a people within an Australian community.

Washing clothes at the same reserve (see p. 104).

Aborigines crossing Apsley Strait in canoes to vote at Bathurst Island, Northern Territory, 1962

It proved more difficult to remove the restrictive laws applying to Aborigines. Long campaigns have been waged by various groups to achieve this, but not until the mid-1960s did much seem to be happening. In various states laws against Aboriginal drinking of alcoholic liquor were relaxed. Aborigines could now travel or marry without government approval. Voting rights were extended. In 1966 the South Australian government granted Aborigines the right to control land reserves, and passed a law to prohibit acts of discrimination against any racial group. In the following year a referendum of the Australian people granted the Commonwealth government much greater power to make laws relating to the Aboriginal people, and decided that Aborigines should be counted in future Commonwealth censuses.

Yet although legal changes were brought about or foreshadowed, Aborigines found the Commonwealth reluctant to seize the opportunity to pass laws for the Aboriginal people, as the 1967 referendum allowed. Nor were restrictive laws entirely abolished. The Queensland Acts of 1965 and 1971 provided for a system whereby Aborigines on reserves remained subject to a number of regulations. These restricted their freedom of expression and decision-making. Ownership of the reserves was not to be in Aboriginal hands, and access to the reserves was restricted. One critic described these restrictions as 'an intolerable invasion of the rights of free movement and freedom of speech and opinion'.

Land Rights

By the 1960s there were signs of angry stirring about the condition of Aboriginal affairs in Australia. Although there were a number of reasons for this, the central issue at that time and since has remained the same—land. The struggle for land rights has come to occupy the most important place in the efforts of Aborigines to improve their position in Australia. This is hardly surprising, considering the traditional importance of land in Aboriginal society. Many white Australians, however, became puzzled and resentful at what they thought was simply a device to get something for nothing.

The land question has not been a simple one. It has often been tied to other matters of great concern to Aborigines. This can be seen in one of the best-known struggles in the recent period—the demand of the Gurindji people of the Northern Territory for the return of their tribal land. In 1966 a large group of Aborigines, basically of Gurindji ancestry, left their camp at Wave Hill station in the Northern Territory and set up a new camp about ten kilometres away. They sought from the controlling British company, Vesteys, an end to low pay, poor food and long hours of work. The new camp was at Daguragu (Wattie Creek) a place full of meaning to them and near other sacred sites of their people. Early in the following year they laid claim to an area of about 1300 square kilometres within the company's leasehold, on which they could establish their own cattle station. A petition was sent to the Governor-General, asking for the return of their land; the Commonwealth government rejected their request, preferring to set up a new township centre at Wave Hill for the Aborigines. But the issue did not die down. Supported by people in the south, many of them white, the Gurindjis kept up their pressure for land. In 1972 some progress came—the government agreed that leases could be available for land for Aborigines, and the company agreed to surrender part of their lease. Yet there were still no rights to own land.

The land rights struggle involved mining companies as well. In 1963 Aborigines at Yirrkala, in north-eastern Arnhem Land, objected to the granting of a lease of part of their reserve to a Swiss company for the mining of bauxite. The Yirrkala sent a petition written on bark to the Commonwealth parliament, claiming the land as part of their own country. It was not something they had ever agreed to grant away. The struggle continued. In 1971 they appealed to the Northern Territory Supreme Court, which declared that there had been no 'civilized' Aboriginal government which owned the land at the time when it was explored and claimed by whites.

Members of a tent embassy talking to Aboriginal Senator Neville Bonner, September 1972. Note the flag

To Aborigines and to an increasing number of whites, the denial of such land rights was simply wrong and unjust. The Yirrkala people protested against the court's decision, presenting a petition to the Prime Minister. They sought ownership of the land and a direct share in royalties from mining on that land. There were other Aboriginal protests over land rights, most dramatically in the setting up of Aboriginal 'embassies'. In Canberra, an Aboriginal tent embassy was set up in 1972 on the lawns of Parliament House. Plainly, not all Aborigines were content with the limited land rights granted to them in some states. It was necessary, they felt, for the Commonwealth to recognize the Aborigines' rights to lands which belonged to their forefathers, and which they had never granted away and could never do so. The Aboriginal leader Bobbi Sykes made clear what was happening:

> The Embassy symbolized that blacks had been pushed as far back as blacks are going to be pushed....First and foremost it symbolized the land rights struggle. But beyond that, it said to white Australia, 'You've kicked us down for the last time.' In all areas. In education, in health, in police victimization, in locking people up en masse—in all these things. It said that blacks were now going to get up and fight back on any or all these issues.[3]

The election of a Federal Labor government in 1972 brought new heart to Aborigines, though not all were happy with some aspects of a new National Aboriginal Consultative Committee and the setting up of a land rights commission, headed by Mr Justice Woodward in 1973–4. The Woodward reports made important recommendations which guided government actions, leading to the Aboriginal Land Rights (Northern Territory) Act in 1976. This Act at last enabled Aborigines in the Territory to have the title to their own land, and to claim vacant Crown land under certain conditions.

Progress on land matters remained uneven, however. There was achievement for the Gurindjis, for at the end of 1974 an agreement was reached about the division of land; in August 1975 Vincent Lingiari, a Gurindji leader, received on behalf of his people the documents for a new Aboriginal pastoral lease. In South Australia an Aboriginal Lands Trust had been set up in 1966, but it was difficult to reach agreement about granting land to Aborigines in the north-west of the state. In February 1980, Pitjantjatjara people travelled by bus to camp in Adelaide and press their case. They finally gained the right to own their reserve land, but Aborigines at Yalata had no such right. Aboriginal ownership of land has for the most part remained a dream. Troublesome disputes made such places as Aurukun and Mornington Island in Queensland and Noonkanbah in Western Australia known

Pitjanjatjara people demonstrating for land rights, at a racecourse in Adelaide

Noonkanbah demonstration, 1981

to many Australians. The problems, often related to mining rights, were made worse by disagreement between the Commonwealth and some state governments. At Noonkanbah in the Kimberley district, Aborigines objected to the granting of a mining lease over their land. In South Australia the government hesitated when it came to the question of surrendering mineral rights. In the Northern Territory, Aboriginal

Land Councils became involved in long negotiations concerning rights to mine uranium and extract oil and gas on traditional Aboriginal land. In other states Aborigines remained dissatisfied about the slow progress towards Aboriginal land ownership. In Queensland and Western Australia, for example, there was resentment at government failure to transfer the title of Aboriginal reserves to Aboriginal Land Trusts, and at other administration of Aboriginal affairs.

Outstations

The Aboriginal desire for a community way of life based on traditional land has been clearly revealed in the outstation movement. During the 1970s there was an increasing flow of Aboriginal people away from townships and reserves to outstations or homeland centres. The movement was strongest in the north and centre of the continent. It was often prompted by a dislike of the pressures and stress in large settlements; it allowed Aborigines greater control over their own affairs and led to more emphasis on gardening, animal raising and the sale of artefacts. Government policy has been to support the movement by the provision of essential services.

Health, Education, Housing, Employment

The outstation movement has kept attention directed on areas of Aboriginal affairs that have been of concern since white settlement first intruded on Aboriginal life. Health is one of these. The ill-health of Aborigines contrasts markedly with their condition before the impact of white people's diseases. Another contrast is with the much lower occurrence of the same diseases among whites in Australia. The fact that the diseases affecting Aborigines are, in the main, preventable and curable has led to much criticism of government efforts and spending in the matter of Aboriginal health.

Many surveys have documented the health problem. Infant mortality in recent decades has remained high. In 1978 deaths among Aboriginal infants in the Northern Territory were still nearly five times higher than among white children, although the total rate was declining. Ear, nose, throat and respiratory infections have been widespread among Aboriginal children, who have also been more likely than white children to experience gastro-enteritis, skin complaints, tooth decay, trachoma and other eye infections. At some settlements in recent years trachoma has occurred among almost all the children. A national report in 1980

Asleep in a dentist's chair—Indulkana, northern South Australia, 1972

A classroom in a modern mission school

emphasized the frequency of the disease, which can cause blindness. Among older Aborigines, leprosy and tuberculosis as well as the above diseases have occurred in high proportions—the incidence of leprosy in the Aboriginal population has given Australia one of the highest rates of this disease in the world. In August 1980 the Department of Aboriginal Affairs reported:

> Aboriginal access to health services at all levels has continued to improve but the general health status of Aboriginals remained markedly below that of the Australian community as a whole.[4]

Similar criticism has been made of education, housing and employment opportunities for Aborigines. Aborigines have had limited opportunities to attend schools and universities. Where they have done so, they have found that education programs have usually ignored Aboriginal culture. From 1970 the Aboriginal Secondary Grants Scheme began to provide assistance for secondary education, and assistance also became available for later training. Of great significance have

Manual arts class,
Maningrida Primary School, N.T.

been the educational efforts to teach Aboriginal languages and culture: bilingual education has thus been provided in a number of remote areas. Other educational measures have been taken. The purpose of such education has also been re-thought. Whites liked to believe that the gaining of educational skills would allow Aborigines to achieve acceptance and equality in the white community. Aborigines have not found this to be so. It is hardly surprising that they have often been more impressed by the educational programs of those remoter schools where pride in Aboriginal identity has been encouraged.

In the matter of housing, conditions for Aborigines have again been far below the general Australian standard. A common sight for decades in Australia has been that of Aborigines living in makeshift accommodation on the edge of towns or at a station camp, Housing on Aboriginal reserves has been little better. A typical example, near Wilcannia in New South Wales in 1965, was described by an observer:

> A dusty track leads you, after a quarter of a mile, into a compound of 14 identical houses, built barracks-like, in two parallel rows . . . . This desert ghetto is the government Aboriginal reserve where 80 people endure a primitive existence without electricity, sinks or baths. Only three houses have stoves . . . . The Aboriginal Welfare Board built this compound and owns the houses, which many of its tenants find most useful for the firewood they provide.[5]

Conditions were no better beyond the reserve. In a deplorable Aboriginal shanty town nearby were more than forty shacks made of bags and tin—they had no water, electricity, stoves or baths. Things were slow to improve: in 1971 a professor of child health described settlement houses near Alice Springs as 'aluminium dog kennels with concrete floors...up to 20 degrees(F) hotter in summer and 20 degrees(F) colder in winter than the rubbish-heap humpy. Most contain no furniture, fireplace or running-water.'[6]

Many houses were built for Aborigines in the 1970s, but there was much left undone or done badly. In 1976, for example, a survey in New South Wales showed that half of that state's Aboriginal people lived in unsatisfactory housing, which was also contributing to poor health. In the following year the Commonwealth Minister for Aboriginal Affairs recognized that houses had often been of poor quality and design, and spoke of 'the appalling housing situation of so many Aboriginal families'.

In employment Aborigines have been handicapped not only by lack of opportunities for necessary training but by very low wages. Only in recent years have Aborigines in several areas of employment become entitled to wages and conditions similar to those of whites, though in some cases it has been possible for employers to evade the requirements

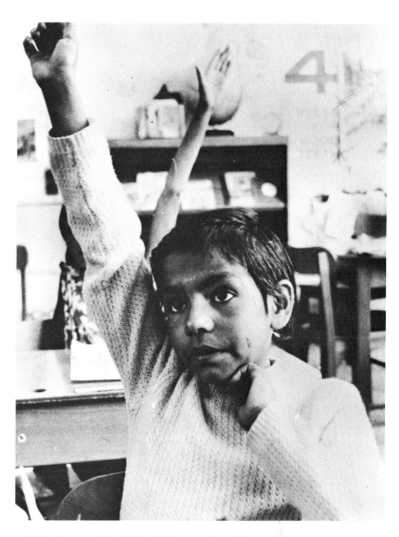

of the law. Aboriginals have found it more difficult than most others to find work in Australia, and unemployment among Aborigines remains several times greater than for the rest of the community. A survey in 1980 showed that Aboriginal unemployment had dramatically worsened in the previous fifteen years. The lives of younger Aborigines in particular have been severely affected. Greater opportunities in the Commonwealth public service have not been able to make a significant difference in the rate of Aboriginal employment.

New Structures

A new vigour became apparent in Aboriginal affairs in the 1970s. Older policies of 'assimilation' had been abandoned. Aborigines wanted a much greater role in determining their own future. White governments tried to further this aim by setting up the National Aboriginal Consultative Committee in 1973, which had only limited success. In 1977 it was

(Opposite top) Aborigines' houses at a government reserve, 1965 (Opposite bottom) Scene on a Western Australian mission station early in the 1970s

Scene in north-western South Australia,
1972

decided to replace it with a new body, the National Aboriginal Conference, an elected body of Aborigines which became much more effective in expressing Aboriginal views. In 1980 the Aboriginal Development Commission was set up: it may acquire land for Aboriginal communities, lend money for housing, personal needs and business undertakings, and advise the federal Minister for Aboriginal Affairs.

'Makarrata'

Progress in solving difficulties between black and white peoples in Australia has often come only after lengthy and bitter negotiation. There have remained the strong sense of injustice and the feeling that disagreements may continue. Perhaps what is needed is more than a new law or laws. It is the end of disputation and the acceptance of normal relations—in Aboriginal language, 'Makarrata'. The term has come to imply a treaty between Aboriginal and white Australians, a treaty within Australia between Australians. By itself, the treaty may not solve problems, but it may express agreement about the rights and proper position of Aborigines in Aus-

A Pitjantjatjara group in August 1972 at
Everard Park station, South Australia.
They told the photographer they wanted
land so they could compete economically
in the white man's world and preserve
the lands of the Dreamtime

A Song of Hope
Look up, my people,
The dawn is breaking,
The world is waking
To a new bright day,
When none defame us,
No restriction tame us,
Nor colour shame us,
Nor sneer dismay.

Now brood no more
On the years behind you,
The hope assigned you
Shall the past replace,
When a juster justice
Grown wise and stronger
Points the bone no longer
At a darker race.

So long we waited
Bound and frustrated,
Till hate be hated
And caste deposed;
Now light shall guide us,
No goal denied us,
And all doors open
That long were closed.

See plain the promise,
Dark freedom-lover!
Night's nearly over,
And though long the climb,
New rights will greet us,
New mateship meet us,
And joy complete us
In our new Dream Time.

To our fathers' fathers
The pain, the sorrow;
To our children's children
The glad tomorrow.

Kath Walker.

tralian society and begin a new relationship between Australians.

The Present and the Future

The new vigour in Aboriginal affairs has owed most to younger Aborigines who are increasingly unable to accept the standards determined for them by the white community. They seek an end to a situation in which their land rights are denied and their opportunities are less than those of white Australians. They have also come to see (though many whites have not) that the problems confronting Aborigines cannot be solved just by government spending of greater amounts of money in the areas in which needs occur. A new awareness of the position of Aborigines and of the nature of Aboriginal society is needed. Aborigines, like racial minorities in other countries, are developing a pride in their own race and their own cultural traditions. Their slogan, too, has become 'Black is beautiful'. They seek an end to the prejudice, and to the mistaken ideas, held by the white community. In many ways this means an end to the Aborigines being regarded as a 'problem'. The truth about which group may be the real problem has been discussed by Professor Tatz:

> When people talk about Aborigines they often ask: 'What's the solution?' 'Solution' suggests there is a 'problem' and those who discuss the 'problem' infer that somehow Aborigines are a naughty, deviant and difficult bunch who have saddled *us* with a problem. If one begins with the idea, as most people do, that Aborigines must be or should be assimilated or integrated, that they must or should adopt our way of life, outlook, culture and values, then there is some truth in the concept of 'problem': the problem of how to change Aborigines, how to devise programmes of social change by what is hideously called social engineering. From an Aboriginal point of view, *we* are the problem: outsiders engaged in trying to re-shape their lives, their attitudes, trying to make them not just plain citizens, but model ones.[5]

In recent decades Aborigines have been able to make whites more aware of the fact that Aborigines as a people do not lack 'ability', as the whites have often claimed. Whites are gradually recognizing that Aboriginal culture is highly developed and extremely complex. At the same time, many Aborigines have excelled in the white man's world—in sport, painting, poetry, and the dramatic arts, for example. Aborigines feel, however, that the real point is not whether they can do the same things as whites—they have positive and distinctive contributions to make in their own way to Australian life and thought. Australia will be much the poorer if these are not made.

Tijina, who had come in from the Gibson
Desert, at Wiluna W. A. 1971.

1 The book by C. D. Rowley, of this title, should be referred to for this and the preceding chapter. See reading list.
2 Quoted in the Sixteenth Annual Report of the Victorian Aboriginal Group, 1945
3 Quoted in Kevin J. Gilbert, *Because a White Man'll Never Do It*, Angus and Robertson Sydney, 1973, p. 29.
4 Department of Aboriginal Affairs — Annual Report 1979–1980, Canberra, 1980, p. 29,
5 *Australian*, 4 January 1965.
6 *Sunday Mail*, 9 October 1971.
7 C. M. Tatz, in *The Aborigine Today*, Sydney, 1971, p. 77.

Reading List

The following is a selection of books which have been published or re-published in recent years and which will be helpful in a further study of Aboriginal life in Australia. They have been divided into two groups, according to chapters in this book.

Chapters 1—3

ABBIE, A. A.: *The Original Australians*, A. H. and A. W. Reed, 1969.

BLAINEY, G.: *Triumph of the Nomads*, Macmillan, 1975.

BERNDT, R. M. and C. H.: *The World of the First Australians*, 2nd edn, Ure Smith, 1977.

BERNDT, R. M. and C. H.: *The First Australians*, 2nd edn., Ure Smith, 1967.

COTTON, B. C. (ed.): *Aboriginal Man in South and Central Australia*, British Science Guild, South Australian Branch, 1966.

EDWARDS, R.: *Aboriginal Bark Canoes of the Murray Valley*, Rigby, 1972.

EDWARDS, R., and GUERIN, B.: *Aboriginal Bark Paintings*, Rigby, n.d.

ELKIN, A. P.: *The Australian Aborigines*, revised edition, Angus and Robertson, 1979.

HAIGH, C. and GOLDSTEIN, W. (eds.): *The Aborigines of New South Wales*, N.S.W. Government National Parks and Wildlife Service, n.d.

HARNEY, W. E.: *Brimming Billabongs*, paperback edn., Rigby, 1969.

HARNEY, W. E., and ELKIN, A. P.: *Songs of the Songmen*, revised edn., Rigby 1968.

MASSOLA, A.: *Journey to Aboriginal Victoria*, Rigby, 1969.

MASSOLA, A.: *The Aborigines of South-Eastern Australia As They Were* Wm. Heinemann, 1971.

McCARTHY, F. D.: *Australian Aboriginal Rock Art*, Australian Museum, Sydney, 1958.

McCARTHY, F. D.: *Australian Aboriginal Decorative Art*, Australian Museum, Sydney, 1962.

McCARTHY, F. D.: *Australian Aboriginal Stone Implements*, Australian Museum, Sydney, 1967.

MOUNTFORD, C. P.: *Brown Men and Red Sand*, Robertson and Mullens, 1948, and later edns.

MULVANEY, D. J.: *The Prehistory of Australia*, revised edition Penguin Books, 1975.

N. J. B. PLOMLEY: *The Tasmanian Aborigines*, The author and Adult Education Division, Tas., 1977.

PRATT B. W. (ed.): *The Australian Encyclopaedia*, Grolier.

REED, A. W.: *An Illustrated Encyclopedia of Aboriginal Life*, A. H. and A. W. Reed, 1969.

ROBERTS, A., and MOUNTFORD, C. P.: *The Dreamtime*, Rigby, 1965, revised 1970.

ROBERTS, A., and MOUNTFORD C. P.: *The Dawn of Time*, Rigby, 1969.

ROBERTS, A., and MOUNTFORD, C. P.: *The First Sunrise*, Rigby, 1971.

WALLACE, P. and N.: *Children of the Desert*, Nelson, 1968.

Chapters 4—5

ADLER, E. et al.: *Justice for Aboriginal Australians*, Australian Council of Churches, Sydney, 1981.

BERNDT, R. M. and C. H. (eds): *Aborigines of the West— Their Past and their Present*, Univ. of W. A. Press, Perth, 1979.

COOMBS, H. C.: *Kulinma—Listening to Aboriginal Australians*, A. N. U. Press, Canberra, 1978.

Current Affairs Bulletins, The University of Sydney.

Department of Aboriginal Affairs, Annual Reports.

ELKIN, A. P. *The Australian Aborigines*, revised edn, Angus and Robertson, 1979.

FRANKLIN, M. A.: *Black and White Australians*, Heinemann Educational, 1976.

GILBERT, K. J.: *Because a White Man'll Never Do It*, Angus and Robertson, 1973.

GILBERT, K. J.: *Living Black*, Penguin, 1978.

HARRIS, S.: *This Our Land*, A. N. U. Press, Canberra 1972.

HARRIS, S.: *'It's Coming Yet...' An Aboriginal Treaty Within Australia Between Australians*, The Aboriginal Treaty Committee, Canberra 1978.

ISAACS, J. (ed.): *Australia's Dreaming 40,000 Years of Aboriginal History*, Lansdowne, Sydney, 1980.

LIPPMAN, L.: *Generations of Resistance The Aboriginal Struggle for Justice*, Longman Cheshire, 1981.

PERKINS, C.: *A Bastard Like Me*, Ure Smith, Sydney, 1975.

PRATT, B. W. (ed.) *The Australian Encyclopaedia*, Grolier.

ROWLEY, C. D.: *The Destruction of Aboriginal Society*, A. N. U. Press, Canberra 1970, and Pelican, 1972 (in the same series, *Outcasts in White Australia* and *The Remote Aborigines*).

SMITH, B.: *The Spectre of Truganini*, A. B. C., 1980.

STANNER, W. E. H.: *After the Dreaming*, A. B. C., 1969.

WILLEY, K.: *When The Sky Fell Down—The Destruction of the Tribes of the Sydney Region 1788–1850s*, Collins, 1979

Research Exercises

Archeology at Koonalda Cave • 1960

A…scientist, sitting one day this month at a stone table in the Nullarbor Plain's Koonalda Cave, realised that an Aborigine had sat there at least 4,000 years ago making flint implements.

The native 'tool factory' had just been uncovered by excavations….

The Koonalda Cave, which in parts extends for 1,600 ft (480 metres), has a ceiling up to 200ft (60 metres) high.

Dr Alexander Gallus…described the discovery in Adelaide at the weekend.

'It was the greatest thrill of our lives suddenly to find this snapshot of interrupted prehistoric activity,' he said.

'The products of this prehistoric workshop, 120 ft(35 metres) below the arid Nullarbor Plain, the stone tools used to make them and the raw material (flint) lay all around, just as the Aboriginal manufacturer had left them.

'In a hollow behind the work-bench lay a fist-size stone hammer of crystalline limestone.

'Apparently it had been used to flake strips from flint, held on a stone work-base, which still lay on the bench.

'A pile of fresh flints, ready for working, lay beside the bench.

'Later excavations to about 4½ ft (1½ metres) in the cave floor revealed stone implements, made there up to about 12,000 years ago.

'This is the only spot in Australia where such an extraordinary sequence of human activity, already extending back to about the end of the Ice Age, has been found.'

The Advertiser, Adelaide, 18 January 1960.

Chapter 1

1 Look up a number of books, including school text books, dealing with the general history of Australia. How much attention and importance does each writer give to the role of the Aboriginal people in that history?
What conclusions can you draw about each writer and his attitude towards the Aborigines?

2 There are a number of books of Aboriginal legends. Refer especially to the books by Ainslie Roberts and C. P. Mountford, *The Dreamtime*, *The Dawn of Time*, and *The First Sunrise*, which contain Aboriginal myths and illustrations referring to the creation period.
What are some of the main features and happenings of that period as revealed in these books?

3 Read the newspaper report on this page about archaeological research.
What do archaeologists try to do?
What do they look for?
What are some of the questions that archaeologists are trying to answer about early Aboriginal life in Australia?
What important discoveries have they been able to make so far about the history of Aborigines in Australia?
Make a diagram or a model in clay of an archaeological digging to illustrate how an archaeologist works. Refer to the illustration on page 3 and to the book by D. J. Mulvaney, *Australian Aboriginal Prehistory*.

4 Write a research report about the Lake Mungo discoveries, giving details of what has been found there. (See in your library the geographical journal *Geo*, Vol. 3, No. 3, 1981, which has a good account and excellent photographs of work at Lake Mungo.) Why are the finds at Lake Mungo really so important?

5 Explain each of the following terms
(a) radio-carbon dating
(b) ice age
(c) firestick farming

6 What various explanations have been given about how Aborigines could have first arrived in Tasmania?

Explain in what ways the Tasmanian Aborig- and their culture differed from the mainland Aborigines and their culture.

7 Can you suggest why the Aborigines were the only residents in Australia for so long?

What can you find out about the Macassan seamen who visited Australia? (Find Macassar on the island of Sulawezi on a map.)

8 In this chapter there has been discussion about what evidence can be found in relation to the Aborigines of earlier times. What evidence survives in your own district concerning former Aboriginal occupation?

What was the name of the tribal group?

What evidence of camp sites can you find? Are there any local names of Aboriginal origin, and what are the meanings of these names?

Have any forms of Aboriginal art or material culture survived?

Chapter 2

1 What were some of the main ways in which the Aborigines adapted to living in the Australian environment?

2 Make a list of methods by which water could be obtained by the Aborigines.

3 Find out what kinds of food were available to Aborigines living under tribal conditions in your locality. (Local histories and museums may help here.) If this cannot be found out exactly, it should be possible to work out what might have been available, basing ideas on the type of country, nearness to rivers or the sea, climate, and other factors. (The article concerning Aborigines in *The Australian Encyclopaedia* should help, and see the list given by the explorer E. J. Eyre below.)

Amongst the almost unlimited catalogue of edible articles used by the natives of Australia, the following may be classed as the chief:—all salt and fresh-water fish and shell-fish, of which, in the larger rivers, there are vast numbers and many species; fresh-water turtle; frogs of different kinds; rats and mice; lizards, and most kinds of snakes and reptiles; grubs of all kinds; moths of several varieties; fungi, and many sorts of

---

roots; the leaves and tops of a variety of plants; the leaf and fruit of the mesembryanthemum; various kinds of fruits and berries; the bark from the roots of many trees and shrubs; the seeds of leguminous plants; gum from several species of acacia; different sorts of manna; honey from the native bee and also from the flowers of the Banksia, by soaking them in water; the tender leaves of the grass-tree; the larvae of insects; white ants; eggs of birds; turtles or lizards; many kinds of kangaroo; opossums; squirrels, sloths, and wallabies; ducks; geese; teal; cockatoos; parrots; wild dogs and wombats; the native companion; the wild turkey; the swan; the pelican; the leipoa, and an endless variety of water-fowl, and other descriptions of birds.

E. J. Eyre: op. cit. pp. 250–1

Discuss the ability of the Aborigines to find food. The following statement, representing the Aboriginal view, should be noted:

Our laws of the dreamtime tell us to hunt all creatures and food by studying their habits and lives. The flowers tell us when to hunt, the traditions of the tribe tell us where we must go to find our food.

…This is our land; it is our flesh and our life, and gives its secrets to those it knows and understands.

W. E. Harney: *Brimming Billabongs*, Adelaide, 1969, p. 50.

4 Make a model of an Aboriginal camp site, using only materials that would have been available to the people (or make a drawing or plan). To do this accurately, find out first what materials would have been used for shelters or huts, where fires would be located in the camp, how many people would have been in it, where weapons would have been evident, etc. (The photograph at the beginning of the book may help.)

5 The accompanying illustration shows the following material objects:

a quartzite knife in a sheath of paper bark, and the same knife withdrawn from the sheath

a hardwood *coolamon* or *pitchi*

a spindle, with string made from human hair

small musical clapping sticks

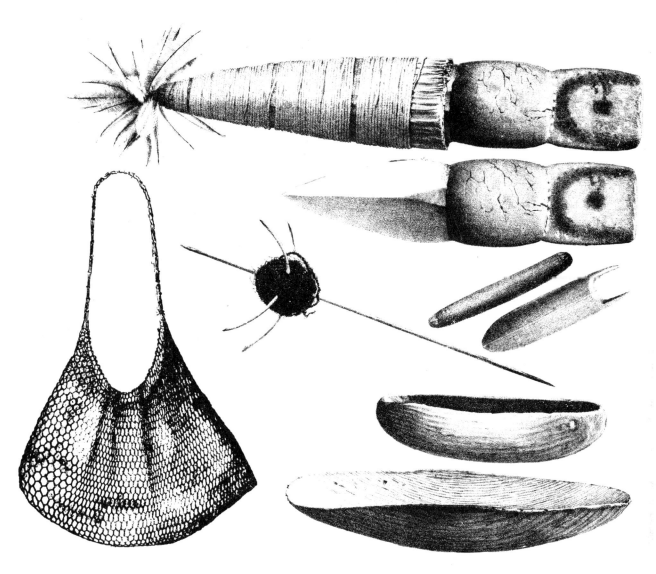

a net bag made from bark fibre, animal fur, or reeds.

What would each of these objects have been used for?

How were the knife and the *coolamon* made? Which material seems to have been of greatest use to Aborigines and why?

6 Read the following statement about Aboriginal trading practices in the Northern Territory, to help answer the question below:

At the big corroborees of the tribes, we would trade with the natives of distant lands, who brought songs as well as goods to exchange. The trade routes were laid down in the dreamtime, and over them come the trading natives at a season when food is plentiful. When the flying-foxes come down the streams from the gorges in the hills and pass the big lily pools in our tribal land, the old men heed the sign, and the tribe moves out to the places where tradition demands that the young men shall be initiated into the secrets of tribal lore.

The tribes would muster at Nuringman, where the trade routes meet at a spot on the Victoria River, for here they had met since the dawn of time. From sunrise way would come the people of Wonga songs, with their special trade of bamboo spears and long throwing sticks. From sundown way would come the natives of the Buradjun songs, with delicately shaped spears fashioned like leaves, and pearl shell pendants called 'jakole' that are said to be the ears

127

of dead Rainbows who dwell in the lands of the big salt waters. From the south would come the tribes of the Iraperinji songs, with stone axes and flaked stone knives with spinifex wax handles. Charrada singing native traders would bring love charms of white clay called 'jerri jerri', and red ochre, and possum aprons for women and men; and the Wallacka natives of the Katherine River side would bring in boomerangs and shields. So also came the natives of Leira, Weba, Jungaree, and Bungal. Each song had its own trade, and the relationship between song and commodity was so fixed in the tribes that the song name really meant the trade goods.

W. E. Harney: *Brimming Billabongs*, p. 64.

What can you find out about Aboriginal trade, the goods and practices traded, and the extent of trade and its importance?
7 How effective were Aborigines in satisfying their material needs?

Chapter 3

1 What were the main characteristics of the period of childhood in Aboriginal life?
2 Find out what you can about each of the following groups—the tribe, the clan, the local group, the elders.
3 Read the following passage:

No English words are good enough to give a sense of the links between an aboriginal group and its homeland. Our word 'home', warm and suggestive though it be, does not match the aboriginal word that may mean 'camp', 'hearth', 'country', 'everlasting home', 'totem place', 'life source', 'spirit centre' and much else all in one. Our word 'land' is too spare and meagre. We can now scarcely use it except with economic overtones unless we happen to be poets. The Aboriginal would speak of 'earth' and use the word in a richly symbolic way to mean his 'shoulder' or his 'side'. I have seen an aboriginal embrace the earth he walked on. To put our words 'home' and 'land' together into 'homeland' is a little better but not much. A different tradition leaves us tongueless and earless towards this other world of meaning and significance. When we took what we call 'land' we took what to them meant hearth, home, the
source and locus of life, and everlastingness of spirit.

W. E. H. Stanner: *After the Dreaming*, Sydney, 1969, p. 44.

From what can be understood about the relationship between the Aborigines and the land, why might an Aborigine embrace the earth, as recorded above?
4 Why did the Aboriginal people hold ritual ceremonies?
5 Read the following statement:

A corroboree was a wild and uninhibited spectacle to a European, but to the participants it was a joyful expression of emotion, a relief from the tedium of daily tasks and at times a prelude to an initiation, increase or other ceremony, or even part of such sacred rites.

A. W. Reed: *An Illustrated Encyclopaedia of Aboriginal Life*, Sydney, 1969, p. 47.

Write an account of an Aboriginal play corroboree, not as a European, but as the participants mentioned above might have described it. Include a description of the musical instruments likely to be involved, the method of making-up the performers, the role of the songman (and perhaps some lines that were sung), the type of actions represented, and the effects on the audience.
6 The accompanying illustration represents a collection of Aboriginal rock paintings. Can you identify the objects painted? (Use your imagination with No. 4! Answers are given on p. R7.
Explain the methods used in rock painting and engraving.
What is the purpose of such art?
7 Discuss some of the questions raised at the end of Chapter 3 p. 71.

Chapter 4

1 Read and discuss the account of Governor Phillip's changing attitude towards the Aborigines in W. E. H. Stanner's *After the Dreaming*, pp. 7–11.
2 What intentions towards the Aborigines are revealed in the following statements made at the beginning of a new Australian colony?

Can you explain why such intentions were not carried out in practice?

Part of the Letters Patent issued by the British government in February 1836 to establish the new province of South Australia:

NOW KNOW YE that…We do hereby erect and establish one Province to be called the Province of SOUTH AUSTRALIA—And we do hereby fix the Boundaries of the said Province…

PROVIDED ALWAYS that nothing in these our Letters Patent contained shall affect or be construed to affect the rights of any Aboriginal Natives of the said Province to the actual occupation or enjoyment in their own persons or in the persons of their descendants of any lands therein now actually occupied or enjoyed by such Natives . . . .

Part of Governor Hindmarsh's First Proclamation to the new colonists in South Australia, December 28 1836:

It is also, at this time especially, my duty to apprise the Colonists of my resolution to take every lawful means for extending the same protection to the NATIVE POPULATION as to the rest of His Majesty's Subjects, and of my firm determination to punish with exemplary severity all acts of violence or injustice which may in any manner be practised or attempted

against the *NATIVES, who are to be considered as much under the Safeguard of the law as the Colonists themselves, and equally entitled to the privileges of British Subjects.*

3 What can you find out about contacts between Aborigines and the early settlers in your own district?

4 The white artist who drew this picture in the middle of the 19th century entitled it simply *Civilisation vs Nature.* What other titles could be given to it, and why?

5 What was the policy of 'soothing the dying pillow'? Why did some whites come to believe in it?

6 Discuss the statement of the Aborigines Progressive Association on p. 102.

Chapter 5

1 Explain the term 'restrictive laws' in regard to Aborigines. What have been some of the criticisms made about these laws?

2 The following map represents Aboriginal population distribution in 1966. What does it reveal?

3 If you were a lawyer presenting a case in favour of land rights for Aborigines, what points would you put forward?

4 Compile a scrap-book of newspaper cuttings relating to Aboriginal affairs.

Identification of rock paintings, Ch. 3, question 6.

1 A dingo (originally drawn in charcoal outline).

2 A snake (shown emerging from a hole).

3 A lizard.

4 An emu sitting on its eggs, as seen from below (a Central Australian painting).

5 A stone knife and handle.

6 Human heads (originally outlined in charcoal).

7 A human hand (an outline formed by blowing charcoal or ochre over the hand).

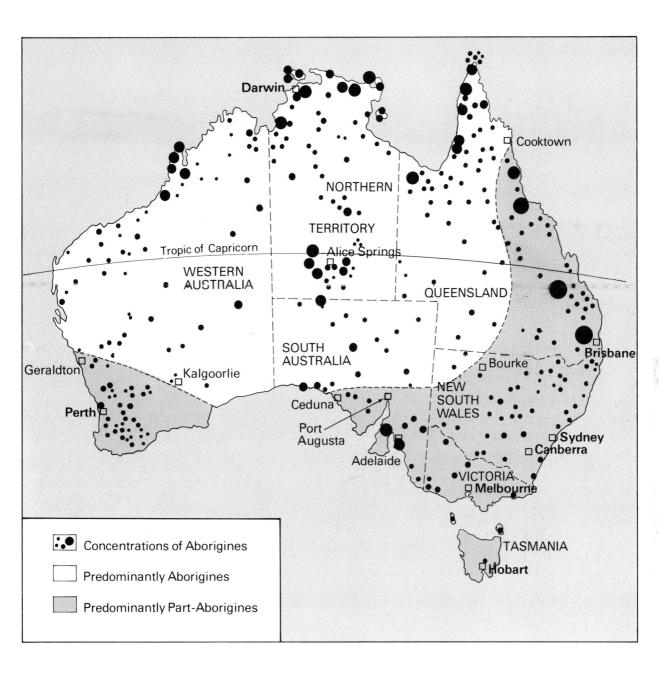

Darwin

NORTHERN
TERRITORY

Cooktown

Tropic of Capricorn

Alice Springs

WESTERN
AUSTRALIA

QUEENSLAND

Geraldton

Kalgoorlie

Perth

SOUTH
AUSTRALIA

Bourke

NEW
SOUTH
WALES

Brisbane

Ceduna

Port
Augusta

Adelaide

Sydney
Canberra

VICTORIA
Melbourne

TASMANIA

Hobart

Concentrations of Aborigines

Predominantly Aborigines

Predominantly Part-Aborigines

Index

Note: References in **bold** type are to illustrations or extracts